Cases

Marbury v. Madison (1803)

McCulloch v. Maryland (1819)

Schenck v. the United States (1919)

Brown v. Board of Education (1954)

Engel v. Vitale (1962)

Baker v. Carr (1962)

Gideon v. Wainwright (1963)

Tinker v. Des Moines Independent Community School District (1969)

New York Times Co. v. United States (1971)

Wisconsin v. Yoder (1972)

Shaw v. Reno (1993)

United States v. Lopez (1995)

McDonald v. Chicago (2010)

Citizens United v. Federal Election Commission (2010)

Marbury v. Madison (1803)

One of the most significant cases in the history of the United States Supreme Court. The ruling in this case established the principle of judicial review—the power of the judiciary to review and invalidate laws and executive actions that it deems unconstitutional. This case essentially set the stage for the Supreme Court to become the final arbiter of the constitutionality of federal laws.

Story of Marbury v. Madison:

The case began with the presidential election of 1800, where Thomas Jefferson, a Democratic-Republican, defeated incumbent President John Adams, a Federalist. Just before Jefferson took office, Adams and the outgoing Federalist Congress passed the Judiciary Act of 1801, which reorganized the federal judiciary and created new courts, judgeships, and judicial positions, including Justice of the Peace positions in the District of Columbia.

Adams, in his last days as president, appointed several Federalists to these positions, including William Marbury as Justice of the Peace in D.C. These last-minute appointments were signed and sealed but had not been delivered by the time Adams left office.

When Jefferson became President, he ordered his Secretary of State, James Madison, not to deliver the commissions. Marbury, whose commission was one of the undelivered ones, petitioned the Supreme Court for a writ of mandamus (a court order) compelling Madison to deliver the commissions.

Chief Justice John Marshall, himself an appointee of Adams, wrote the Court's opinion. He reasoned that while Marbury was entitled to his commission, the Court could not grant the requested mandamus. Marshall stated that the portion of the Judiciary Act of 1789 that gave the Supreme Court the power to issue such a writ was unconstitutional, as it extended the Court's original jurisdiction beyond what was envisaged in Article III of the Constitution.

Why it's important:

This case is important because, in ruling the Judiciary Act of 1789 was unconstitutional, the Supreme Court effectively gave itself the power of judicial review. This power allows the judiciary to review and invalidate laws and executive actions that it deems unconstitutional. This principle has been a cornerstone of U.S. law and has shaped the balance of power among the three branches of government.

Cases that use Marbury v. Madison as a precedent:

Marbury v. Madison has been cited in numerous cases to affirm the principle of judicial review. Here are a few significant ones:

McCulloch v. Maryland (1819): This case used Marbury as a precedent to assert the Supreme Court's power to interpret the Constitution and determine the constitutionality of an act of Congress (in this case, the creation of a national bank).

Dred Scott v. Sandford (1857): This controversial case saw the Court use its power of judicial review to declare the Missouri Compromise unconstitutional.

Brown v. Board of Education (1954): In this landmark case, the Supreme Court declared state laws establishing separate public schools for black and white students to be unconstitutional, again asserting its power of judicial review.

Key terms and concepts for Marbury v. Madison (1803):

- Judicial review: The power of courts to declare laws and actions of local, state, or national government invalid if they violate the Constitution.
- Writ of mandamus: A court order compelling someone to execute a duty that they are legally obligated to complete.
- Judiciary Act of 1789: A U.S. federal statute that established the structure and jurisdiction of the federal court system and created the position of the attorney general.

McCulloch v. Maryland (1819)

Landmark decision by the Supreme Court of the United States that solidified the principle of implied powers (Necessary and Proper Clause) of the federal government. The case also reaffirmed the supremacy of federal law over state law when the two conflict (Supremacy Clause).

Background and Decision:

In 1816, Congress chartered The Second Bank of the United States. In 1818, the state of Maryland passed legislation to impose taxes on the bank. James W. McCulloch, the cashier of the Baltimore branch of the bank, refused to pay the tax.

The legal issue that the case presented was: Does the Constitution grant the federal government the power to establish a bank, even though that power is not specifically listed in the Constitution? And, do individual states have the power to tax a federally established entity?

The Court, led by Chief Justice John Marshall, decided that the federal government had the right to establish the bank. Although the Constitution does not specifically give the federal government the authority to establish a bank, it does grant it the implied powers necessary to implement its enumerated powers. In this case, establishing the bank was seen as necessary and proper to carry out the government's enumerated powers related to taxation and the regulation of currency.

Furthermore, the Court held that Maryland's tax on the bank was unconstitutional because federal law is supreme over state law. A state cannot use its taxing power to challenge the constitutionally granted powers of the federal government.

Importance:

McCulloch v. Maryland is significant because it established two important principles in constitutional law. First, the decision affirmed the "necessary and proper" clause of the Constitution, giving Congress implied powers that allow it to implement its enumerated powers. Second, it reaffirmed the principle of federal supremacy, meaning that state laws cannot interfere with federal laws.

Precedent:

McCulloch v. Maryland has been used as a precedent in a large number of cases, as its central principles are fundamental to the structure of American federalism. Here are some of the most important cases that have used it as a precedent:

Gibbons v. Ogden (1824): This case extended the federal government's powers to regulate interstate commerce.

Dartmouth College v. Woodward (1819): This case applied the principle of federal supremacy to protect contracts against interference by state governments.

South Dakota v. Dole (1987): This case upheld the federal government's power to indirectly encourage uniformity in states' drinking ages by withholding federal highway funds from states that did not raise their drinking age to 21.

National Federation of Independent Business v. Sebelius (2012): This case upheld most of the Affordable Care Act. Chief Justice John Roberts' opinion discussed the Necessary and Proper Clause and referenced McCulloch v. Maryland extensively.

Gonzales v. Raich (2005): This case upheld the application of the Controlled Substances Act to homegrown marijuana, citing the federal government's broad power under the Commerce Clause and the Necessary and Proper Clause.

Key terms for understanding McCulloch v. Maryland (1819):

Federalism: A system of government in which power is divided between a central (national) government and smaller political units, such as states.

Implied powers: Powers not explicitly named in the Constitution but assumed to exist due to their being necessary to implement the expressed powers.

Necessary and Proper Clause (Elastic Clause): A clause in the U.S. Constitution that gives Congress the power to make all laws that are necessary and proper for carrying out its duties.

Supremacy Clause: A clause in the U.S. Constitution stating that federal law takes precedence over state laws.

National bank: A financial institution chartered and regulated by the federal government, and historically in the U.S., often debated over the implied powers of the Constitution.

Schenck v. United States (1919)

Schenck v. United States was a landmark Supreme Court case that helped define the limits of the First Amendment's protection of free speech. The case arose during World War I when Charles Schenck, the secretary of the Socialist Party of America, was arrested and convicted for distributing 15,000 leaflets urging people to resist the draft.

Schenck argued that his conviction was a violation of his First Amendment rights to free speech. However, the Supreme Court, led by Justice Oliver Wendell Holmes Jr., unanimously upheld his conviction. The Court argued that in times of war, the government has a greater interest in maintaining order and security.

Justice Holmes articulated what became known as the "clear and present danger" test. He wrote: "The most stringent protection of free speech would not protect a man from falsely shouting fire in a theater and causing a panic. [...] The question in every case is whether the words used are used in such circumstances and are of such a nature as to create a clear and present danger that they will bring about the substantive evils that Congress has a right to prevent."

Why It's Important

Schenck v. United States established the "clear and present danger" test, a significant legal concept used to balance the First Amendment rights and the government's interest in maintaining security and order. It has influenced many later decisions related to free speech, especially those involving national security.

Cases Using Schenck as Precedent

Abrams v. United States (1919): This case involved Russian immigrants who were convicted for distributing leaflets that criticized U.S. intervention in the Russian Revolution. The Supreme Court upheld the convictions using the "clear and present danger" test.

Dennis v. United States (1951): This case concerned leaders of the Communist Party of the USA who were convicted under the Smith Act of 1940 for conspiring to teach or advocate the overthrow of the government by force. The Court upheld the convictions, modifying the "clear and present danger" test into a "gravity of the 'evil,' discounted by its improbability" formula.

Brandenburg v. Ohio (1969): This case overturned the conviction of a Ku Klux Klan leader under an Ohio criminal syndicalism law. The Court introduced a new standard—the "imminent lawless action" test—that further narrowed the circumstances under which speech can be lawfully restricted. This case effectively replaced the "clear and present danger" test with a more protective standard for free speech.

Elois v. U.S. (2015): The U.S. Supreme Court in an 8-1 opinion reversed a trial court conviction of a man found guilty under a federal stalking statute on the grounds that the man was convicted under instructions that required only that the jury find that he communicated what a reasonable person would regard as a threat. Anthony Douglas Elonis was prosecuted after he had posted on Facebook rap lyrics under the name of "Tone Dougie" that appeared to threaten his ex-wife, an FBI agent and a kindergarten class. He had included disclaimers indicating that his lyrics were "fictitious," that they were "therapeutic," that they emulated the lyrics of rap star Eminem, and that they were a proper exercise of Elonis' First Amendment rights.

At trial, Elonis requested the judge to instruct the jury that to convict him, the government must prove that he intended to convey a true threat. Instead, the court instructed jurors that they need only find that "a reasonable person" would interpret the words to constitute such a threat. The reasonable person standard reduced the standard for a criminal conviction to that of negligence, which is more consistent with the standard for civil liability, not a criminal conviction.

Key terms for understanding Schenck v. United States (1919):

First Amendment: The amendment to the U.S. Constitution that guarantees freedoms concerning religion, expression, assembly, and the right to petition.

Freedom of speech: The right to express any opinions without censorship or restraint.

Clear and present danger test: A doctrine adopted by the Supreme Court of the United States to determine under what circumstances limits can be placed on First Amendment freedoms of speech, press, or assembly.

Espionage Act of 1917: A United States federal law passed shortly after entering World War I, making it a crime for a person to convey information with intent to interfere with the operation or success of the armed forces of the United States or to promote the success of its enemies.

Brown v. Board of Education (1954)

Brown v. Board of Education (1954) was a landmark United States Supreme Court case that fundamentally reshaped the nation's approach to racial segregation in public schools. Here's a summary of the case:

Background:
In the early 1950s, racial segregation was still widespread in public schools across the United States, particularly in the Southern states. The case originated from a lawsuit filed by the parents of African American students, including Oliver Brown, who challenged the segregated school system in Topeka, Kansas. The plaintiffs argued that the policy of racial segregation violated the constitutional rights of their children.

Court Decision:
The Supreme Court, led by Chief Justice Earl Warren, issued a unanimous decision in favor of the plaintiffs, overturning the "separate but equal" doctrine established by the Plessy v. Ferguson case (1896). The Court held that racial segregation in public education facilities was inherently unequal and violated the Equal Protection Clause of the Fourteenth Amendment to the United States Constitution.

Impact: Brown v. Board of Education had far-reaching consequences for American society and the civil rights movement. It laid the groundwork for desegregating public schools and challenged the notion of racial segregation in all aspects of American life. The decision marked a significant step toward dismantling legal racial discrimination and promoting equal educational opportunities for all races.

Overturned: Plessy v. Ferguson (1896): Brown v. Board of Education explicitly overturned the "separate but equal" doctrine established in Plessy v. Ferguson, which had permitted racial segregation in various public facilities, including schools.

Cases for Which Brown v. Board Has Been Used as Precedent:

1. Cooper v. Aaron (1958): The Supreme Court reaffirmed the principles and holding of Brown v. Board of Education, stating that its decision was binding on all states and that compliance was mandatory.
2. Green v. County School Board of New Kent County (1968): The Court used Brown v. Board of Education as precedent to strike down "freedom of choice" plans used to circumvent desegregation orders.

3. Swann v. Charlotte-Mecklenburg Board of Education (1971): The Court applied the principles of Brown v. Board of Education to establish the use of busing and other measures to achieve school desegregation.

These are just a few examples of cases where Brown v. Board of Education has been used as precedent. Its impact extends beyond the realm of education and has influenced subsequent civil rights litigation and efforts to combat racial discrimination in various contexts.

Terms for understanding Brown v. Board of Education (1954):

Equal Protection Clause: Part of the 14th Amendment to the U.S. Constitution, this clause prohibits states from denying any person within its jurisdiction the equal protection of the laws. It states: "No State shall deny to any person within its jurisdiction the equal protection of the laws." The clause was ratified in 1868 following the American Civil War and was intended to ensure equal treatment and rights for all individuals under the law.

The Equal Protection Clause is a significant constitutional provision that aims to prevent states from enacting laws or engaging in actions that discriminate against individuals or groups based on certain characteristics such as race, ethnicity, gender, religion, or national origin. Its purpose is to guarantee that all people are treated fairly and equally by the government. It prohibits intentional discrimination, but also covers cases of unintentional or indirect discrimination that result in unjustifiable inequalities.

Over the years, the Equal Protection Clause has been influential in various landmark Supreme Court cases, including Brown v. Board of Education (1954) and Obergefell v. Hodges (2015), which legalized same-sex marriage nationwide. These decisions have expanded the application of the clause to protect various marginalized groups and ensure equal treatment under the law.

Fourteenth Amendment: An amendment to the U.S. Constitution that grants citizenship to "all persons born or naturalized in the United States," including formerly enslaved people, and provides all citizens with "equal protection under the laws."

"Separate but equal" doctrine: The doctrine established by the U.S. Supreme Court in Plessy v. Furgeson (1898) that racial segregation was constitutional as long as the separate facilities provided for blacks and whites were equal in quality.

Engel v. Vitale (1962)

Landmark Supreme Court case decided in 1962 that declared school-sponsored prayer in public schools to be unconstitutional. This case played a significant role in the application of the Establishment Clause of the First Amendment to the United States Constitution, which states, "Congress shall make no law respecting an establishment of religion..."

Story of Engel v. Vitale:
In the early 1960s, the New York State Board of Regents had authorized a short, voluntary prayer for recitation at the start of each school day. This prayer was non-denominational and intended to be a statement of moral, spiritual, and patriotic values. However, a group of families in Hyde Park, NY, led by Steven Engel, objected to this practice, arguing that it violated the Establishment Clause of the First Amendment, which prohibits the government from making any law "respecting an establishment of religion."

The case eventually made its way to the Supreme Court. In a 6-1 decision, the Court agreed with Engel, ruling that the prayer, even if non-denominational and voluntary, constituted an unlawful religious exercise by the state. The Court held that by providing the prayer, New York officially approved religion, which was a violation of the Establishment Clause. This was the first in a series of cases in which the Court used the establishment clause to eliminate religious activities of all sorts, which had historically been a part of public ceremonies.

Why It's Important
Engel v. Vitale is important because it significantly broadened the interpretation of the Establishment Clause, applying it to state as well as federal actions (due to the incorporation doctrine). The decision emphasized a strict separation of church and state, meaning that the government could not sponsor religious activities or favor any one religion.

Cases That Use Engel v. Vitale as a Precedent

School District of Abington Township, Pennsylvania v. Schempp (1963): The Supreme Court ruled that Bible readings in public schools were a violation of the Establishment Clause, citing Engel v. Vitale as a precedent.

Lemon v. Kurtzman (1971): This case further expanded on Engel's Establishment Clause ruling, leading to the creation of the "Lemon Test" to determine when a law has the effect of establishing religion. The Lemon test is a legal framework developed by the United States Supreme Court in the case of Lemon v. Kurtzman (1971) to determine the constitutionality of laws or government actions that potentially violate the Establishment Clause of the First Amendment. The Establishment Clause prohibits the government from making any law "respecting an establishment of religion."

The Lemon test consists of three prongs that must be satisfied for a law or government action to be considered constitutional under the Establishment Clause:

1. The law or action must have a secular (non-religious) purpose[1]. This prong requires that the primary purpose of the law or action is secular rather than religious. It aims to prevent the government from favoring or endorsing any particular religion.
2. The law or action must neither advance nor inhibit religion. It prohibits the government from excessively entangling itself in religious matters or showing favoritism toward any religious group.
3. The law or action must not result in excessive entanglement between government and religion. It aims to maintain a separation between the institutions of government and religion.

To pass the Lemon test, a law or government action must meet all three prongs. If any prong is violated, the law or action is considered to violate the Establishment Clause. The Lemon test has been influential in shaping the Supreme Court's decisions on cases involving government support for religious activities, such as public funding for religious schools or displays of religious symbols on public property.

Stone v. Graham (1980): The Court, citing Engel, struck down a Kentucky statute requiring the posting of the Ten Commandments in public school classrooms.

Lee v. Weisman (1992): The Supreme Court held that school-sponsored prayer at graduation ceremonies violated the Establishment Clause, relying partly on Engel v. Vitale.

Key terms for understanding Engel v. Vitale (1962):
Prayer in school: The controversial practice of reciting prayers in public schools, often seen as a violation of the Establishment Clause.

State-sponsored prayer: A government-endorsed prayer, which is often considered a violation of the Establishment Clause of the First Amendment.

---

[1] "Secular" refers to things that are not religious or not related to religious or spiritual matters. It refers to a worldview, perspective, or approach that is independent of religious beliefs or affiliations. Secular can be used to describe various aspects of society, government, education, or individuals that are free from religious influence or bias.

Separation of church and state: The principle that the government must maintain an attitude of neutrality toward religion. Many view such separation as necessary to the freedom of religion.

Text of prayer challenged in Engel: 'Almighty God, we acknowledge our dependence upon Thee, and we beg Thy blessings upon us, our parents, our teachers and our Country. '

The prayer is said upon the commencement of the school day, immediately following the pledge of allegiance to the flag.

Baker v. Carr (1962)

Landmark United States Supreme Court case that decided that redistricting (attempts to change how a state is divided into political districts) issues present justiciable questions, thus enabling federal courts to intervene in and decide redistricting cases.

The Story of Baker v. Carr

The case was brought forward by Charles Baker, a Republican from Tennessee, who noticed a lack of redistricting efforts in his state despite significant population shifts. The Tennessee constitution required that districts be redrawn every decade according to the federal census to provide for districts of substantially equal population. However, Tennessee had not redistricted since 1901, and urban areas, despite their larger populations, did not have proportional representation compared to rural areas.

Baker sued Joe Carr, the state official responsible for elections, arguing that the lack of redistricting violated the Equal Protection Clause of the 14th Amendment because it devalued his vote.

The case made its way to the Supreme Court, and the primary question was whether the Court could rule on this issue, as it raised questions about the "political question doctrine," which is the idea that some matters are more appropriately dealt with by elected branches, not courts.

In a 6-2 decision, the Supreme Court held that federal courts have the power to rule on the constitutionality of state apportionment (distribution of voters into districts) processes. This ruling meant that Baker's claim was justiciable, and it could proceed in court.

Why It's Important

Baker v. Carr is considered a landmark case because it paved the way for the "one person, one vote" doctrine, which requires electoral districts to be roughly equal in population. The ruling also established the justiciability of issues related to the apportionment of state legislative districts, which was a significant step in making federal courts a venue for redistricting battles.

Important Cases That Use It as Precedent

Reynolds v. Sims (1964): This case directly built on "Baker v. Carr" and established the "one person, one vote" doctrine, ruling that state legislative districts must be roughly equal in population. The decision was based on the Equal Protection Clause of the 14th Amendment.

Wesberry v. Sanders (1964): This case extended the "one person, one vote" principle to U.S. Congressional districts, requiring each state to draw districts with equal populations.

Shaw v. Reno (1993): This case used the precedent set by "Baker v. Carr" to decide that redistricting based on race must be held to a standard of strict scrutiny under the Equal Protection Clause. The decision in this case continued to define the rules for redistricting and gerrymandering.

Gill v. Whitford (2018): This more recent case involved claims of partisan gerrymandering in Wisconsin. The Court did not decide on the merits of the claims but sent the case back to the lower court to establish whether plaintiffs had sufficient standing. The case demonstrated the ongoing complexity and contention around redistricting, with "Baker v. Carr" as a foundational precedent.

Key terms for understanding Baker v. Carr (1962):

Political question doctrine: A principle used by courts to decline hearing a case if they believe it should be dealt with through the legislative or executive branch, not the judicial.

Redistricting: The process of redrawing electoral district boundaries in order to achieve relatively equal populations within each district.

Apportionment: The process of allotting congressional seats to each state following the decennial census according to their proportion of the population.

"One person, one vote": A principle meaning that election districts should have equal populations so that one person's voting power is roughly equivalent to another person's within the state.

Census: The census plays a crucial role in congressional districting, which is the process of dividing a state into different electoral districts for the purpose of electing representatives to the United States House of Representatives. The census provides important data on population distribution and demographics that inform the redrawing of district boundaries. A census is taken every 10 years. The last census was taken in 2020.

Here's how the census influences congressional districting:

1. Population Allocation: The census collects data on the population of each state, including demographic information such as age, race, and ethnicity. This data is used to determine each state's representation in the House of Representatives. The total population count helps determine the number of seats each state receives, based on the principle of "one person, one vote."

2. Apportionment: After the census is conducted, the U.S. Census Bureau determines the reapportionment of House seats among the states. The total number of seats in the House (435) remains fixed, but their distribution among the states can change based on population shifts. States that have gained population relative to others may gain seats, while those with declining populations may lose seats. This reallocation is done to ensure fair representation based on population changes over time.

3. Redistricting: Once the apportionment process is completed, states are responsible for redrawing their congressional district boundaries. Redistricting is typically carried out by state legislatures or independent redistricting commissions. The census data, including population counts and demographic information, is crucial in this process. The goal is to create districts of roughly equal population size to uphold the principle of "one person, one vote" and ensure that each district has roughly the same number of constituents.

The census data helps determine the ideal population size for each district, and redistricting aims to achieve equal representation and prevent the dilution of minority voting power. It also takes into consideration requirements set by federal and state laws, such as respecting existing geographic boundaries, avoiding gerrymandering (manipulating district boundaries to favor a particular political party), and complying with the Voting Rights Act, which protects the rights of minority voters.

Gideon v. Wainwright (1963)

Landmark Supreme Court case in American legal history that fundamentally transformed the country's criminal justice system. The case centered on the Sixth Amendment's right to counsel clause, specifically its application in state courts.

The Story:

Clarence Earl Gideon was a poor drifter accused in Florida of felony theft. Because Gideon could not afford a lawyer, he asked the judge to appoint one for him. The judge denied his request, citing Florida law that only provided counsel for poor defendants in capital cases. Gideon was left to defend himself at trial, which resulted in a guilty verdict and a five-year prison sentence.

While in jail, Gideon studied law and filed a handwritten petition to the Supreme Court arguing that he was denied his Sixth Amendment right to counsel, a right that he believed was "fundamental and essential to a fair trial."

The Ruling and Its Importance:

In a unanimous decision, the Supreme Court ruled in Gideon's favor. The Court held that the Sixth Amendment's right to counsel was a fundamental right and essential to a fair trial, and that states are required under the Fourteenth Amendment to provide counsel in criminal cases to represent defendants who are unable to afford to pay their own attorneys.

The decision in Gideon v. Wainwright is considered a landmark because it greatly expanded the rights of accused individuals and fundamentally transformed American criminal justice. It established the principle that a person who cannot afford to hire an attorney must be appointed one by the state - this principle is now a well-known part of the "Miranda rights" read to individuals upon arrest.

Precedents:

Gideon v. Wainwright has been used as a precedent in numerous subsequent cases. Here are some of the most significant:

Argersinger v. Hamlin (1972): This case extended the right to counsel for any defendant, regardless of the severity of the crime, who is charged with an offense punishable by imprisonment.

Alabama v. Shelton (2002): This case extended the right to counsel to defendants in cases where the defendant is given a suspended sentence that may result in incarceration if the terms of the sentence are violated.

Rothgery v. Gillespie County (2008): The Supreme Court ruled that a person's Sixth Amendment right to counsel attaches at their initial appearance before a judicial officer, and they do not need to be "prosecuted," i.e., have a prosecutor involved, for this right to apply.

Key terms for understanding Gideon v. Wainwright (1963):

Sixth Amendment: Part of the U.S. Constitution's Bill of Rights that sets forth rights related to criminal prosecutions, including the right to a fair and speedy trial, to counsel, and to confront one's accusers.

Right to counsel: The legal responsibility for the government to provide every defendant in a criminal trial the ability to have a lawyer.

Due Process Clause: Found in both the Fifth and Fourteenth Amendments, it prohibits governmental deprivations of "life, liberty, or property" without due process of law.

Incorporation doctrine: The constitutional doctrine whereby selected provisions of the Bill of Rights are made applicable to the states through the Due Process clause of the Fourteenth Amendment.

Indigent defendants: Individuals in criminal court proceedings who lack the means to pay for a private attorney and are therefore entitled to a public defender or appointed counsel.

Writ of certiorari: a legal order issued by a higher court, typically an appellate court, to review and reconsider a case that has been decided by a lower court. It is commonly used in the context of the United States Supreme Court, where it is an essential mechanism for the Court to select cases for its review.

When a party to a case is dissatisfied with the decision of a lower court, they may petition the higher court for a writ of certiorari. However, the higher court has the discretion to grant or deny the writ. If the writ is granted, it means that the higher court agrees to review the case and consider whether the lower court's decision was correct.

Tinker v. Des Moines (1969)

Landmark Supreme Court case that established a precedent for students' rights to free speech in schools. The case centered on a group of students who were suspended from school for wearing black armbands in protest of the Vietnam War. The Supreme Court ruled in favor of the students, stating that students do not "shed their constitutional rights to freedom of speech or expression at the schoolhouse gate."

Story of Tinker v. Des Moines

In December 1965, a group of students in Des Moines, Iowa, decided to wear black armbands to their schools (elementary and high schools) as a silent protest against the Vietnam War. The students were part of a larger anti-war movement and chose to wear these armbands as a symbol of mourning for the lives lost in the war. The students planned to wear the armbands until New Year's Day.

The principals of the Des Moines school district became aware of the plan and, fearing that it might cause a disruption, met on December 14, 1965, and created a policy that any student wearing an armband would be asked to remove it, and refusal to do so would result in suspension.

Despite the policy, Mary Beth Tinker (13 years old), her brother John Tinker (15 years old), and their friend Christopher Eckhardt (16 years old) wore their black armbands to school. When asked to remove them, they refused and were subsequently suspended. The students did not return to school until after New Year's Day, in accordance with their original protest plan.

The students, through their parents, filed a lawsuit claiming that their First Amendment rights had been violated. The case went through several courts, with the District Court ruling in favor of the school district and the U.S. Court of Appeals for the Eighth Circuit affirming the decision without opinion.

Precedents for Tinker v. Des Moines:

West Virginia State Board of Education v. Barnette (1943): This case set the precedent that the government could not force individuals, including students, to salute the flag or say the pledge of allegiance. The Court affirmed that these were forms of symbolic speech protected under the First Amendment.

Brown v. Board of Education (1954): While not directly about free speech, this case established the principle of equal protection under the law for students in public schools. This case helped to lay the groundwork for protecting students' rights, including free speech.

Cases for which "Tinker v. Des Moines" was a precedent:

Bethel School District No. 403 v. Fraser (1986): In this case, the Supreme Court ruled that a school could discipline a student for giving a lewd speech during a school assembly, limiting the free speech rights established in Tinker. The Court held that the rights of students in public schools are not automatically coextensive with the rights of adults in other settings.

Hazelwood School District v. Kuhlmeier (1988): This case further limited the Tinker precedent by ruling that schools have the right to regulate certain types of speech in school-sponsored activities, like student newspapers, if they have a legitimate pedagogical concern.

Morse v. Frederick (2007): In this case, the Supreme Court ruled that a school could suspend a student for displaying a banner ("Bong Hits 4 Jesus") at a school-sanctioned event because it could reasonably be viewed as promoting illegal drug use. This further limited the Tinker precedent.

Mahanoy Area School District v. B.L. (2023) When 14-year-old Brandi Levy did not make her public school's varsity cheerleading team. Levy expressed her disappointment on the social-media app Snapchat by posting a photo in which she had her middle finger raised, with the caption "F— school f— softball f— cheer f— everything." Although Levy's snap was only visible for 24 hours to 250 of her friends, coaches saw screenshots of the post and she was suspended from the junior varsity team for a year on the grounds that the post violated team and school rules. Levy went to court, where she argued that the suspension violated the First Amendment. When the lower courts agreed, the school district went to the Supreme Court, which in January agreed to weigh in. The court's opinion was by Justice Stephen Breyer, who wrote that – unlike the U.S. Court of Appeals for the 3rd Circuit – the majority did not believe that "the special characteristics that give schools additional license to regulate speech always disappear when a school regulates speech that takes place off campus." The school may have a substantial interest in regulating, Breyer suggested, a variety of different kinds of off-campus conduct – for example, severe bullying, threats aimed at teachers or students, participation in online school activities or hacking into school computers.

Key terms for Tinker: Symbolic speech: Actions that purposefully and discernibly convey a particular message or statement to those viewing it.

New York Times Co. v. United States (1971)

Also known as the "Pentagon Papers Case," was a landmark decision by the United States Supreme Court on the First Amendment. The case affirmed the prohibition of prior restraint—pre-publication censorship—in most instances.

In 1971, Daniel Ellsberg, a former Defense Department worker, leaked a top-secret study detailing the U.S. government's military involvement in Vietnam from 1945 to 1967. This study, later known as the Pentagon Papers, revealed that the government had misled the public about the scale and purpose of its operations in Vietnam. The New York Times and The Washington Post sought to publish the contents of these documents. The Nixon Administration attempted to prevent this, arguing that its publication would interfere with the country's foreign policy and national defense.

The case quickly escalated to the Supreme Court, which had to decide whether the constitutional freedom of the press, guaranteed by the First Amendment, was subordinate to a claimed need of the executive branch of government to maintain the secrecy of information.

In a 6-3 decision, the Supreme Court ruled that the government had failed to justify restraint of publication. The Court held that any system of prior restraints comes to the Court bearing a heavy presumption against its constitutional validity. The government "thus carries a heavy burden of showing justification for the imposition of such a restraint."

The case is crucial as it established the high bar the government would have to clear to justify any form of prior restraint on expression. It reaffirmed the central role of the press in a democratic society and its function as a watchdog on government power.

Cases where New York Times Co. v. United States was used as precedent:

1. Nebraska Press Association v. Stuart (1976): This case involved a court order restraining the press from publishing or broadcasting accounts of confessions made by the accused to the police. The Supreme Court held that the order violated the First and Fourteenth Amendments, citing the "Pentagon Papers Case" to assert that prior restraint on media is highly suspect and bears a heavy presumption against its constitutional validity.

2. The Progressive Case (United States v. The Progressive, Inc.) in 1979: The government tried to use prior restraint to stop the publication of an article in The Progressive magazine that purportedly contained information on how to make a hydrogen bomb. Citing the Pentagon Papers case, the court initially sided with the government. Still, the case was later dropped when similar information was published elsewhere, making the restraint moot.

3. Landmark Communications, Inc. v. Virginia (1978): The Supreme Court overturned a conviction of a newspaper for publishing confidential information from a judicial review commission, holding that neither the Commonwealth's interest in protecting the confidentiality of proceedings nor its interest in maintaining the integrity of its judiciary was sufficient to justify the subsequent punishment of accurate news reporting.

Key terms in understanding New York Times Co. v. United States (1971):

Freedom of the press: The right to circulate opinions in print without censorship by the government.

Prior restraint: Censorship imposed, usually by a government or institution, before a speech, film, book, etc., is made public.

Pentagon Papers: Secret U.S. Defense Department study of U.S. political and military involvement in Vietnam from 1945 to 1967, leaked to the press by Daniel Ellsberg.

National security: The requirement to maintain the survival of the state through the use of economic power, diplomacy, power projection, and political power.

Wisconsin v. Yoder (1972)

Landmark United States Supreme Court case that dealt with the constitutional right to freedom of religion. The case was decided on May 15, 1972.

Background and Decision:

In the state of Wisconsin, compulsory school attendance was required for all children until age 16. However, a group of Amish parents refused to send their children to school past the eighth grade, arguing that high school attendance was contrary to their religious beliefs.

The parents were prosecuted under Wisconsin law, but they contended that their First Amendment right to free exercise of religion was being violated by the compulsory attendance law. The case eventually made its way to the Supreme Court.

In a unanimous decision, the Supreme Court held that an individual's rights under the Free Exercise Clause of the First Amendment outweighed the State's interests in compelling school attendance beyond the eighth grade. The Court found that the values and programs of secondary school were in sharp conflict with the fundamental mode of life mandated by the Amish religion.

Importance:

The decision in Wisconsin v. Yoder is significant because it established a precedent for religious exemptions to generally applicable laws, and it upheld the right of parents to direct their children's education in line with their religious beliefs.

The case is often cited in discussions about the balance between an individual's right to free exercise of religion and the state's interest in a specific regulation. It's particularly important in cases involving compulsory education laws and religious beliefs.

Cases Using Wisconsin v. Yoder as Precedent:

Employment Division v. Smith (1990): This case dealt with the use of peyote, a hallucinogenic drug, in Native American religious ceremonies. The Supreme Court held that a state could deny unemployment benefits to a person fired for violating a state prohibition on the use of peyote, even though the use of the drug was part of a religious ritual. Although the decision in Smith significantly narrowed the scope of religious exemptions to generally applicable laws, Wisconsin v. Yoder was distinguished as a case where the Court had found a violation of the Free Exercise Clause.

Church of the Lukumi Babalu Aye v. City of Hialeah (1993): This case involved a Santeria church that performed animal sacrifices as part of its religious rituals. The city passed ordinances prohibiting such sacrifices, and the Supreme Court held that the ordinances violated the Free Exercise Clause. The Court cited "Wisconsin v. Yoder" in its discussion of religious freedom.

Key terms in understanding Wisconsin v. Yoder (1972):

Free Exercise Clause: The section of the First Amendment that protects the right to practice one's religion without government interference.

Compulsory school attendance: Laws that require a person to go to school starting between 5 and 8 years of age, and continuing until they are between 16 and 18 years old.

Amish: An Anabaptist Christian denomination known for simple living, plain dress, and reluctance to adopt many conveniences of modern technology.

Shaw v. Reno (1993)

Landmark Supreme Court case that addresses the issue of racial gerrymandering, the practice of manipulating electoral districts to favor one race or class.

Story of Shaw v. Reno

In North Carolina after the 1990 census, the state was given an additional seat in the House of Representatives due to an increase in population. The state legislature created a district that was predominantly African American, which was approved by the Department of Justice. However, the state created a second district, District 12, that was also majority African American. District 12 was unusually shaped, stretching approximately 160 miles along Interstate 85 and, at some points, was no wider than the highway itself. The shape of the district led to accusations that it was an example of racial gerrymandering.

Five white North Carolina residents, led by Ruth O. Shaw, challenged the constitutionality of District 12. They argued that the district was created solely based on race, which violated their Fourteenth Amendment right to equal protection under the law.

In a 5-4 decision, the Supreme Court ruled in favor of Shaw. The Court held that redistricting based on race must be held to a standard of strict scrutiny under the equal protection clause. This means that such redistricting must serve a compelling government interest and must be narrowly tailored to meet that interest. The ruling didn't eliminate the potential for race to be considered in the formation of districts, but it set a higher standard for its use.

Importance of Shaw v. Reno

1. Racial Gerrymandering: It addressed the concept of racial gerrymandering and established that districts cannot be drawn solely based on race.

2. Strict Scrutiny: It set a precedent that racial gerrymandering cases are subject to strict scrutiny, the highest standard of review.

3. Equal Protection: It upheld the principle that the Fourteenth Amendment's Equal Protection Clause applies to redistricting.

Cases Using Shaw v. Reno as Precedent

Some important cases that have used "Shaw v. Reno" as precedent:

Miller v. Johnson (1995): This case furthered the precedent set in Shaw v. Reno. In this case, the Court ruled that a Georgia congressional district was unconstitutional because its boundaries were determined predominantly by race.

Hunt v. Cromartie (2001): This case showed the complexity of the issue. The Supreme Court ruled that North Carolina's 12th district wasn't unconstitutional because, while race was a factor in its creation, it was not the predominant factor. The Court showed that political motives could be a legitimate reason for creating a strangely shaped district.

Alabama Legislative Black Caucus v. Alabama (2015): The Court ruled that the state of Alabama's redistricting plan, which packed black voters into certain districts, could not be justified by the Voting Rights Act, continuing the precedent of Shaw v. Reno that race can't be the predominant factor in redistricting.

Key terms in understanding Shaw v. Reno (1993):

Racial gerrymandering: The deliberate manipulation of legislative district boundaries to disadvantage or favor one racial or ethnic group over others.

Voting Rights Act of 1965: This is a landmark piece of federal legislation in the United States that prohibits racial discrimination in voting. It was designed to enforce the voting rights guaranteed by the Fourteenth and Fifteenth Amendments to the United States Constitution.

Majority-Minority Districts: These are electoral districts (such as U.S. congressional districts) in which the majority of the constituents in the district are racial or ethnic minorities. The creation of such districts during redistricting can be controversial, as in the case of Shaw v. Reno, and can be perceived as racial gerrymandering.

Equal Protection Clause: The part of the Fourteenth Amendment to the U.S. Constitution that prohibits states from denying any person within its jurisdiction the equal protection of the laws. This was a key concept in the Shaw v. Reno case, as the Court found that North Carolina's redistricting plan violated the Equal Protection Clause because it segregated voters into separate districts based on race.

Strict Scrutiny: This is the most stringent standard of judicial review used by United States courts. It is part of the hierarchy of standards that courts use to weigh the government's interest against a constitutional right or principle. Under this standard, the government must show that its law or policy is necessary to achieve a compelling state interest, and is narrowly tailored to achieving that interest. In Shaw v. Reno, the Supreme Court applied strict scrutiny to the redistricting plan.

Race-Based Redistricting: The practice of drawing district lines to include or exclude individuals based on their race. In Shaw v. Reno, the Supreme Court ruled that race-based redistricting must be held to a standard of strict scrutiny under the equal protection clause.

United States v. Lopez (1995)

Landmark case in U.S. constitutional law that centered on the Commerce Clause of the Constitution, which allows the federal government to regulate interstate commerce.

The Story:

In 1992, a 12th-grade student named Alfonso Lopez, Jr., brought a concealed handgun to his high school in San Antonio, Texas. He was charged under Texas law with firearm possession on school premises. However, the next day, federal agents charged Lopez with violating the Gun-Free School Zones Act of 1990, a federal law that made it illegal for any individual knowingly to possess a firearm at a place that the individual knows, or has reasonable cause to believe, is a school zone. The federal charges led to the state charges being dismissed.

Lopez's defense attorney moved to dismiss the indictment, arguing that the Act was unconstitutional as it was beyond the power of Congress to legislate control over public schools. The motion was denied, and Lopez was convicted. The case made its way through the courts, eventually reaching the Supreme Court.

The Supreme Court Decision:

In a 5-4 decision, the Supreme Court ruled in favor of Lopez. Chief Justice Rehnquist, writing for the majority, argued that while Congress had broad lawmaking authority under the Commerce Clause, the power was limited and did not extend so far from "commerce" as to authorize the regulation of the carrying of handguns, especially when there was no evidence of any sort of economic enterprise.

Why It's Important:

United States v. Lopez is a landmark case because it was the first time in over half a century that the Supreme Court set limits to Congress's power under the Commerce Clause. The decision emphasized that the clause did not give Congress a blank check to regulate any activity that might conceivably affect commerce.

Cases Using United States v. Lopez as Precedent:

United States v. Morrison (2000): The Supreme Court struck down the federal civil remedy provision of the Violence Against Women Act of 1994, again arguing that it exceeded Congress's power under the Commerce Clause. The "Lopez" decision was used as a precedent, showing a continuing trend toward limiting the use of the Commerce Clause to justify federal jurisdiction in areas traditionally controlled by the states.

Gonzales v. Raich (2005): Although the Court upheld the federal regulation of home-grown marijuana as within Congress's power under the Commerce Clause, the dissenting opinions by Justices O'Connor and Thomas cited "Lopez" and "Morrison" as evidence that the Court was extending the Commerce Clause too far.

Lopez changes application of the Commerce Clause:

"Heart of Atlanta Motel, Inc. v. United States" (1964) and "United States v. Lopez" (1995) are both significant cases related to the interpretation of the Commerce Clause of the U.S. Constitution, but they actually provide contrasting perspectives.

In "Heart of Atlanta Motel, Inc. v. United States," the Supreme Court upheld the constitutionality of the Civil Rights Act of 1964, ruling that Congress could use its power under the Commerce Clause to enforce the Act's prohibition of discrimination in public accommodations. The motel argued that its business was of a local character, but the Court found that the motel's operations affected interstate commerce because it catered to interstate travelers.

In contrast, "United States v. Lopez" marked a shift in the Court's interpretation of the Commerce Clause. The case involved a federal law prohibiting the possession of a firearm in a school zone. The Supreme Court held that the law exceeded Congress's Commerce Clause power, reasoning that possession of a gun in a local school zone was not an economic activity that substantially affects interstate commerce.

"Heart of Atlanta Motel" is a precedent in the sense that it was a previous decision involving the Commerce Clause, but the decision in "Lopez" did not directly rely on the "Heart of Atlanta Motel" decision. Rather, "Lopez" signaled a shift towards a more limited interpretation of the Commerce Clause. However, the contrast between these cases shows the evolution and fluctuation in the Court's interpretation of the Commerce Clause over time.

"Heart of Atlanta Motel" established the broad reach of the Commerce Clause in regulating a wide range of activities, even those seeming local in nature, that have a substantial effect on interstate commerce. "Lopez" began to put some limits on that reach, emphasizing that not all local activities can be said to have the requisite connection to interstate commerce for federal regulation.

Key terms for understanding United States v. Lopez (1995):

Commerce Clause: The section of the Constitution which gives Congress the power to regulate trade among the states and with foreign countries.

Gun-Free School Zones Act: A federal act that bans possessing firearms in a school zone. The law applies to public, private, and parochial elementary schools and high schools, and to non-private property within 1000 feet of them.

The 10th Amendment and constitutional limits on federal power: The Tenth Amendment of the U.S. Constitution reads: "The powers not delegated to the United States by the Constitution, nor prohibited by it to the States, are reserved to the States respectively, or to the people."

Reserved Powers: The decision can be seen as reinforcing the Tenth Amendment's reservation of powers to the states. By striking down the Act, the Court suggested that regulating guns in school zones was a matter more suited for local or state laws rather than federal legislation. This is because public education and the safety of school children are typically considered to fall under the police power of the states, which is a power reserved to them by the Tenth Amendment.

McDonald v. City of Chicago (2010)

Landmark decision by the Supreme Court of the United States that determined whether the Second Amendment applies to the individual states. The case came about after Chicago resident Otis McDonald, along with other plaintiffs, filed a lawsuit against the city's handgun ban, arguing that it violated their Second Amendment rights to keep and bear arms.

The Second Amendment, part of the Bill of Rights, traditionally applied only to the federal government, not the states. However, the 14th Amendment, ratified after the Civil War, extended the Bill of Rights' protections to the state level. The "Due Process" and "Privileges or Immunities" clauses of the 14th Amendment were intended to prevent states from infringing upon the rights of citizens.

In a 5-4 decision, the Supreme Court ruled that the Second Amendment right to keep and bear arms for self-defense is fully applicable to the states through the 14th Amendment. This was a significant extension of the Court's decision in "District of Columbia v. Heller" (2008), which had affirmed an individual's right to possess a firearm unconnected with service in a militia and to use that firearm for traditionally lawful purposes, like self-defense within the home. However, Heller didn't explicitly extend these rights to the states.

Why is McDonald v. Chicago important?

1. Incorporation Doctrine: The ruling in McDonald v. Chicago applied the Incorporation Doctrine to the Second Amendment, meaning that the protections offered by the Second Amendment were now applicable to the states, not just the federal government.

2. Impact on Gun Control Laws: By extending Second Amendment rights to the state level, the McDonald decision set a precedent that could be used to challenge state and local gun control laws across the country.

The cases "District of Columbia v. Heller" (2008) and "McDonald v. City of Chicago" (2010) are landmark decisions in U.S. Supreme Court jurisprudence on the Second Amendment, which protects the right to keep and bear arms.

In "Heller," the Supreme Court held for the first time that the Second Amendment protects an individual's right to possess a firearm unconnected with service in a militia and to use that firearm for traditionally lawful purposes, such as self-defense within the home. This ruling directly contradicted the collective rights theory, which held that the Second Amendment protects a collective right of states to maintain militias, but not an individual right to own guns. Prior to "Heller," this theory had been influential in many lower court rulings and had been suggested in the Supreme Court case of "United States v. Miller" (1939), although "Miller" did not definitively resolve the individual versus collective rights issue.

In "McDonald v. City of Chicago," the Supreme Court extended the "Heller" decision to the states, ruling that the Second Amendment is incorporated by the Due Process Clause of the Fourteenth Amendment and thus applies to state and local governments, as well as the federal government. This ruling contradicted earlier decisions in some lower courts that had held the Second Amendment did not apply to the states.

While "Heller" and "McDonald" did not explicitly overrule any specific Supreme Court decisions, they marked significant shifts in the Court's interpretation of the Second Amendment. They effectively reversed a long-standing trend in many courts to interpret the Second Amendment as protecting a right connected with militia service, rather than an individual right to gun ownership.

Key terms in understanding McDonald v. City of Chicago (2010):

Second Amendment: Part of the U.S. Constitution that protects the individual's right to keep and bear arms.

Gun control laws: Laws or policies that regulate the manufacture, sale, transfer, possession, modification, or use of firearms.

Militia: In the context of the Second Amendment to the U.S. Constitution, the term "militia" has been subject to much debate. Historically, it referred to a group of citizens who are not professional soldiers but can be called upon for military service in times of emergency. The Second Amendment reads, "A well regulated Militia, being necessary to the security of a free State, the right of the people to keep and bear Arms, shall not be infringed." The interpretation of this wording, and specifically the phrase "well regulated Militia," was a central issue in D.C. v. Heller, which held that the Second Amendment protects an individual's right to possess a firearm unconnected with service in a militia, and to use that firearm for traditionally lawful purposes, such as self-defense within the home.

Citizens United v. Federal Election Commission (2010)

Landmark U.S. Supreme Court case concerning campaign finance.

Background: Citizens United, a conservative non-profit organization, sought to air and advertise a film critical of Hillary Clinton in close proximity to the 2008 Democratic primary. However, doing so would violate the Bipartisan Campaign Reform Act (BCRA), also known as the McCain-Feingold Act, which prohibited corporations (including non-profit corporations) and unions from funding "electioneering communications" (broadcast ads referring to a candidate) within 30 days of a primary or 60 days of a general election.

Decision: In a 5-4 ruling, the Supreme Court held that the BCRA's restrictions on corporate and union funding of independent political broadcasts in candidate elections violated the First Amendment's guarantee of Freedom of Speech. The court argued that political spending is a form of protected speech under the First Amendment, and the government may not keep corporations or unions from spending money to support or denounce individual candidates in elections.

Significance: The decision effectively overturned two previous rulings: Austin v. Michigan Chamber of Commerce (1990), which upheld restrictions on corporate spending to support or oppose political candidates, and parts of McConnell v. Federal Election Commission (2003), which upheld the portion of the BCRA at issue. The ruling also paved the way for unlimited election spending by corporations and unions and led to the creation of Super PACs (Political Action Committees), which can raise and spend unlimited amounts of money to advocate for or against political candidates.

Cases where "Citizens United v. Federal Election Commission" served as a precedent:

SpeechNow.org v. Federal Election Commission (2010): Following the Citizens United ruling, the U.S. Court of Appeals for the D.C. Circuit held that limits on contributions to groups that make only independent expenditures are unconstitutional, leading to the rise of Super PACs.

McCutcheon v. Federal Election Commission (2014): This Supreme Court decision struck down the aggregate limits on the amount an individual may contribute during a two-year period to all federal candidates, parties, and political action committees combined. The court held that the First Amendment does not permit the government to restrict how much a person donates to such groups, so long as the donations are disclosed.

American Tradition Partnership, Inc. v. Bullock (2012): This Supreme Court decision struck down a Montana state law that restricted corporate political expenditures, reinforcing the Citizens United decision at the state level.

These cases and others have relied on Citizens United as a major precedent in campaign finance law, with significant impacts on the financing of political campaigns in the U.S.

The Citizens United case, officially known as Citizens United v. Federal Election Commission, was a landmark Supreme Court case in the United States that addressed campaign finance regulations and political spending. The case was decided in 2010 and set significant precedents regarding political contributions and the role of corporations in elections.

Here are some key precedents relevant to the Citizens United case:

1. Buckley v. Valeo (1976): In this case, the Supreme Court established that spending money on political campaigns is a form of protected free speech under the First Amendment. It recognized the importance of protecting political speech and struck down certain restrictions on campaign expenditures while upholding certain limitations on campaign contributions.

2. First National Bank of Boston v. Bellotti (1978): The Court held that corporate political speech is protected under the First Amendment. It allowed corporations, like individuals, to engage in political speech and spend money on ballot initiatives.

3. Austin v. Michigan Chamber of Commerce (1990): The Court upheld a state law that prohibited corporations from using their general treasury funds to make independent expenditures in support of or opposition to political candidates. It allowed the government to regulate corporate political spending to prevent corruption or the appearance of corruption.

4. McConnell v. Federal Election Commission (2003): This case involved the Bipartisan Campaign Reform Act of 2002 (also known as McCain-Feingold Act). The Court upheld certain restrictions on campaign finance, including limits on political contributions and restrictions on corporate and union-funded issue ads within a specific time frame before elections.

5. Citizens United v. Federal Election Commission (2010): The case at the center of this question, Citizens United, overturned certain aspects of the McConnell decision. The Court held that restrictions on independent political spending by corporations, labor unions, and certain other organizations violated their First

Amendment rights. It concluded that political spending is a form of protected speech, and the government cannot suppress speech based on the identity of the speaker. The decision removed limits on independent expenditures by corporations and unions, allowing them to spend unlimited amounts on political advertisements.

The Citizens United case was significant in reshaping the campaign finance landscape in the United States. It led to the rise of Super PACs (Political Action Committees) and increased the influence of money in politics by allowing corporations and unions to spend unlimited funds on independent political advertisements, leading to debates about the potential for undue influence and the balance between free speech and the integrity of elections.

Roe v. Wade (1973)

Landmark decision by the United States Supreme Court on the issue of abortion. The case was decided in 1973 and is one of the most well-known and significant cases in U.S. legal history due to its impact on women's reproductive rights.

The case originated when an unmarried pregnant woman, known under the pseudonym "Jane Roe" (real name Norma McCorvey), challenged the constitutionality of the Texas law that made it a crime to perform an abortion unless a woman's life was at stake. The defendant was Henry Wade, the district attorney of Dallas County, where Roe resided.

In a 7-2 decision, the Supreme Court held that a woman's right to choose to have an abortion fell within the right to privacy, which was protected by the Fourteenth Amendment. The Court acknowledged that this right was not absolute and had to be balanced against the state's two legitimate interests for regulating abortions: protecting prenatal life and protecting the woman's health. It established a trimester framework to balance these interests. In the first trimester, a state could not regulate abortion beyond requiring that it be performed by a licensed doctor in medically safe conditions. In the second trimester, a state could regulate abortion if the regulations were reasonably related to the health of the pregnant woman. In the third trimester, after the fetus is viable outside the womb, a state could regulate or even prohibit abortion, except in cases where it was necessary to protect the life or health of the woman.

The significance of "Roe v. Wade" lies in its affirmation of a constitutional right to privacy and the recognition of a woman's right to make certain fundamental decisions about her own body and personal life. This case effectively legalized abortion across the United States.

Important cases that have used "Roe v. Wade" as a precedent:

Planned Parenthood v. Casey (1992): This is perhaps the most important case that followed "Roe v. Wade." In "Casey," the Supreme Court reaffirmed the basic ruling of "Roe" that the Constitution protects a woman's right to make her own decision about abortion. However, the court discarded Roe's trimester framework and instead adopted an "undue burden" standard for determining whether a state's abortion restrictions were constitutional.

Whole Woman's Health v. Hellerstedt (2016): This case further clarified the "undue burden" standard from "Casey." The Supreme Court invalidated two provisions of a Texas law that required doctors who perform abortions to have admitting privileges at a nearby hospital and required abortion clinics to have facilities comparable to an ambulatory surgical center. The court ruled that these requirements placed a substantial obstacle in the path of women seeking an abortion and constituted an undue burden on abortion access.

Dobbs v. Jackson Women's Health Organization was a landmark 2022 decision addressing whether the Constitution protects the right to an abortion. In Dobbs, the Supreme Court reviewed the constitutionality of Mississippi's Gestational Age Act—a law banning most abortions after 15 weeks of pregnancy with exceptions for medical emergencies and fetal abnormalities. In a divided opinion, the Court upheld the Mississippi law and overturned Roe v. Wade (1973) and Planned Parenthood v. Casey (1992)—concluding that the Constitution does not protect the right to an abortion. As a result, the Court's decision returned the issue of abortion regulation to the elected branches. In an opinion concurring in the judgment, Chief Justice Roberts agreed to uphold the Mississippi law, but chided the majority for reaching out to decide the broader question of whether to overrule Roe and Casey. He would have left that important constitutional question to a future case. Finally, in a rare joint dissent, Justices Breyer, Kagan, and Sotomayor criticized the Court for unsettling nearly five decades of precedent and undermining the Constitution's promise of freedom and equality for women.

Key terms in understanding Roe v. Wade (1973):

Abortion: The deliberate termination of a human pregnancy, most often performed during the first 28 weeks of pregnancy.

Right to privacy: The concept that one's personal information is protected from public scrutiny. U.S. Justice Louis Brandeis called it "the right to be left alone." While not explicitly stated in the U.S. Constitution, some amendments provide some protections, and it has been inferred by the courts from several of the amendments in the Bill of Rights.

Penumbra of Rights: The concept that the Constitution's explicit rights have "penumbras", or zones, that protect related rights. This is drawn from the idea that constitutional rights cast "shadows" of protection that cover areas not specifically mentioned in the constitution.

Ninth Amendment: The Ninth Amendment states that the enumeration in the Constitution, of certain rights, shall not be construed to deny or disparage others retained by the people. This has been interpreted as justification for broadly reading the Bill of Rights to protect privacy in ways not specifically provided in the first eight amendments.

Fourteenth Amendment: This amendment to the U.S. Constitution, among other things, prohibits states from denying any person life, liberty or property without due process of law, or denying to any person within its jurisdiction the equal protection of the laws.

Trimester: A period of three months, particularly the divisions of pregnancy into three three-month periods.

Viability: The point in a pregnancy when a fetus could survive outside the uterus, generally agreed to be at about 24 weeks gestation.

Roe v. Wade overturned in 2022:

Dobbs v. Jackson Women's Health Organization is the 2022 Supreme Court case that reversed Roe v. Wade and Planned Parenthood of Southeastern Pennsylvania v. Casey, the decisions that originally asserted the fundamental right to an abortion prior to the viability of the fetus. Dobbs v. Jackson states that the Constitution does not confer a right to abortion; and, the authority to regulate abortion is "returned to the people and their elected representatives."

Facts:
The case involved Mississippi's Gestational Age Act, passed in 2018, which prohibited abortions after 15 weeks except for medical emergencies or severe fetal abnormalities. The act also applied penalties such as license suspension to abortion providers. Consequently, Jackson Women's Health organization filed suit in a federal district court and challenged the constitutionality of the Gestational Age Act. Thomas Dobbs (the petitioner) was a Mississippi State Health officer. Dobbs filed a petition for certiorari, which was granted. The Supreme Court granted writ to address whether all pre-viability prohibitions on elective abortions are unconstitutional.

Arguments:
Mississippi, through Dobbs, argued that the Constitution does not provide a right to abortion (and as such, states can freely ban abortions if it is rationally related to legitimate government interests). Mississippi leaned on the text of the Tenth Amendment, that denies states powers like making treaties, but does not directly deny the power to restrict abortion. Additionally, Mississippi argued that "liberty" as written in the Fourteenth Amendment only implicates fundamental rights that are "deeply rooted in U.S history and tradition." Mississippi further argued that abortion is not a fundamental right here since many states at the time of the Fourteenth Amendment's ratification had bans on abortions. Additionally, Mississippi contended that the "viability line" prevented a state from protecting its interest and was too arbitrary or subjective.

In contrast, Jackson's Women's Health Organization ("Women's Health") argued that abortion is grounded in the Fourteenth Amendment. It asserted that physical autonomy and body integrity are "essential elements of liberty protected by the Due Process Clause." For example, contraception is included in the word "liberty." Women's Health also argued that abortion, or the right of a person to have possession of their own body is important in the common law tradition. Furthermore, Women's Health pointed out that federal courts have uniformly applied the viability line.

Decision:

Justice Alito wrote the majority opinion, joined by Justices Thomas, Gorsuch, Kavanaugh, and Barrett. The Court explained that the critical question was whether the Constitution "properly understood" confers a right to obtain an abortion. The Court first stated that the Constitution makes no express references to abortion. Further, Court precedent holds that a state regulation of abortion is not a sex-based classification (and so is not subject to heightened scrutiny).

From there, the Court then established that abortion is not deeply rooted in the Nation's history and traditions. The Court elaborated that the Due Process Clause protects only two types of substantive rights, rights guaranteed by the first eight Amendments, and rights that are deemed fundamental. As such, The Court noted that the history of abortion in the U.S is "as a crime"-- that at the time the Fourteenth Amendment was adopted, three-quarters of the States had made abortion a crime at any stage of pregnancy. The Court explained that this was true until Roe v. Wade—and thus, "liberty" would not recognize abortion as a fundamental right rooted in the nature, history, or traditions of the nation. Indeed, the Court stated that "Roe either ignored or misstated this history."

The Court also explained that "the people of various states" may evaluate the interests between "potential life" and a "woman who wants an abortion" differently than the Court. Finally, the Court concluded that abortion is not part of a broader entrenched right—that justifying this premise "proves too much." The Court said that linking abortion to a right to autonomy or to "define one's concept of existence" would also license fundamental rights to "illicit drug use, [or] prostitution."

Implications:

Now that abortion is not awarded the status of a fundamental right, rational-basis review is the standard used when looking at state abortion regulations that undergo a constitutional challenge. Essentially, States may regulate abortion "for legitimate reasons" and if those laws are challenged under the Constitution, they are entitled to "a strong presumption of validity."

Federalism

Federalism, as a fundamental principle of the U.S. government, establishes the distribution and balance of power between the central, national government and its constituent units at the state and local levels. It's a distinctive feature of the U.S. political system and plays a crucial role in how the Constitution is interpreted and applied.

Supreme Court cases that demonstrate the principle of federalism:

McCulloch v. Maryland (1819): This case is a pillar of federal supremacy. The Court upheld that the Constitution grants Congress implied powers to execute its express powers and that state action may not obstruct valid constitutional exercises of power by the Federal government.

Baker v. Carr (1962): The Supreme Court asserted the federal judiciary's authority to intervene in state affairs concerning the apportionment of electoral districts. The Court established the "one person, one vote" principle, thereby asserting federal power over state voting laws.

Shaw v. Reno (1993): This case involved allegations of racial gerrymandering, and the Court's decision emphasized the federal government's role in overseeing state redistricting plans to ensure they comply with the Equal Protection Clause. The case demonstrated that while states have primary responsibility for drawing congressional districts, the federal courts have a role in preventing racial discrimination in the redistricting process.

United States v. Lopez (1995): This case marked a shift in the trend of expanding federal power under the Commerce Clause. The Court decided that Congress had overstepped its constitutional authority by passing a law that criminalized gun possession near schools, an issue typically regulated at the state and local levels.

Brown v. Board of Education (1954): In this landmark case, the Supreme Court ruled that segregated public schools violated the Equal Protection Clause, thereby invalidating the "separate but equal" doctrine. This case underscored the federal government's role in addressing racial injustices, even those perpetuated by state or local governments.

McDonald v. City of Chicago (2010): Here, the Supreme Court affirmed that the Second Amendment right to keep and bear arms for self-defense applies to the states through the Fourteenth Amendment, demonstrating the incorporation doctrine's role in extending federal constitutional protections at the state level.

Gideon v. Wainwright (1963): This case embodies the principle of "incorporation," in which provisions of the Bill of Rights are applied to the states through the Due Process Clause of the Fourteenth Amendment. This case resulted in increased uniformity in the criminal justice system across states by mandating that all states provide counsel in criminal cases, regardless of a defendant's ability to pay.

Each of these cases offers insights into the balance of power between the federal and state governments and how this balance can shift based on interpretations of the U.S. Constitution. They collectively showcase the principle of federalism in action within the U.S. legal system.

Civil rights and civil liberties

Civil rights and civil liberties are fundamental concepts in U.S. law, but they refer to different kinds of protections.

Civil rights refer to the rights of individuals to receive equal treatment (and to be free from unfair treatment or discrimination) in a number of settings, including education, employment, housing, and more, and are based on certain legally-protected characteristics. They're generally associated with policies of non-discrimination and equal treatment.

Civil liberties, on the other hand, refer to constitutional freedoms guaranteed to all citizens, often spelled out in the Bill of Rights, such as freedom of speech, the right to bear arms, the right against self-incrimination, or the right to a fair trial.

Civil Rights Cases:

- Baker v. Carr (1962): This case addressed the civil right of political participation, as it ruled that the federal courts have the authority to enforce the principle of "one person, one vote," ensuring equal representation.

- Shaw v. Reno (1993): This case addressed racial gerrymandering, highlighting the civil right to participate in the political process without experiencing discrimination based on race.
- Brown v. Board of Education (1954): This landmark case addressed the civil right to equal protection under the law, ruling that racial segregation in public schools was unconstitutional.

-Brown v. Board of Education (1954) is generally considered a civil rights case rather than a civil liberties case. The case was a landmark Supreme Court decision that declared state laws establishing separate public schools for Black and white students to be unconstitutional, thereby overturning the "separate but equal" doctrine established by the Plessy v. Ferguson case in 1896.

Brown v. Board of Education primarily addressed the issue of racial segregation in public schools, highlighting the violation of the Equal Protection Clause of the Fourteenth Amendment. The decision emphasized that separate educational facilities based on race inherently created inequalities and infringed upon the rights of African American students to equal educational opportunities.

While the case does involve the protection of civil liberties, such as the right to education, it is generally categorized as a civil rights case due to its focus on combating racial discrimination and promoting equality under the law. The decision in Brown v. Board of Education was a significant step towards dismantling racial segregation and promoting civil rights for African Americans in the United States.

Civil Liberties Cases:

-In Schenck v. United States, the Supreme Court ruled that the First Amendment does not protect speech that presents a "clear and present danger" to the government or public welfare. The case established the "clear and present danger" test, which became a significant precedent for evaluating the limits of free speech.
- Tinker v. Des Moines Independent Community School District (1969): This case protected the civil liberty of free speech, establishing that students do not lose their constitutional rights when they enter a school.
- New York Times Co. v. United States (1971): This case protected the civil liberty of the press, allowing them to publish classified documents without risk of government censorship or punishment, establishing what's known as the "Pentagon Papers" ruling.
- Engel v. Vitale (1962): This case addressed the civil liberty of religious freedom, ruling that government-directed prayer in public schools violates the Establishment Clause of the First Amendment.
-Gideon v. Wainwright (1963): This case is also viewed as a civil liberties case. The decision is grounded in the Sixth Amendment's guarantee of the right to counsel in criminal prosecutions. The Supreme Court ruled that this right is so fundamental that if a defendant cannot afford an attorney, the state must provide one. Thus, the decision focused on the individual's liberty to have fair legal representation, which is a fundamental civil liberty protected by the Constitution.
- Wisconsin v. Yoder (1972): This case protected the civil liberty of religious freedom, recognizing the right of parents to withdraw their children from school for religious reasons.
- Citizens United v. Federal Election Commission (2010): This case addressed the civil liberty of free speech, ruling that corporations have a First Amendment right to expressly support political candidates for Congress and the White House.
-Roe v. Wade (1973): This case is generally considered a case about civil liberties. The Supreme Court's decision in Roe was primarily based on the Constitution's implicit right to privacy. The right to privacy is considered a civil liberty 'liberty' that the government may not infringe upon. In this case, that right was extended to a woman's decision to have an abortion. The Court held that a state law that banned abortions (except to save the life of the mother) was unconstitutional and that women have the constitutional right to choose whether to have an abortion.

DOCUMENTS

The Declaration of Independence

The Articles of Confederation

The Constitution

Federalist Paper 10

Federalist Paper 51

Federalist Paper 70

Federalist Paper 78

Brutus 1

Letter from a Birmingham Jail

The Declaration of Independence

In Congress, July 4, 1776

The unanimous Declaration of the thirteen united States of America, When in the Course of human events, it becomes necessary for one people to dissolve the political bands which have connected them with another, and to assume among the powers of the earth, the separate and equal station to which the Laws of Nature and of Nature's God entitle them, a decent respect to the opinions of mankind requires that they should declare the causes which impel them to the separation.

We hold these truths to be self-evident, that all men are created equal, that they are endowed by their Creator with certain unalienable Rights, that among these are Life, Liberty and the pursuit of Happiness.--That to secure these rights, Governments are instituted among Men, deriving their just powers from the consent of the governed, --That whenever any Form of Government becomes destructive of these ends, it is the Right of the People to alter or to abolish it, and to institute new Government, laying its foundation on such principles and organizing its powers in such form, as to them shall seem most likely to effect their Safety and Happiness. Prudence, indeed, will dictate that Governments long established should not be changed for light and transient causes; and accordingly all experience hath shewn, that mankind are more disposed to suffer, while evils are sufferable, than to right themselves by abolishing the forms to which they are accustomed. But when a long train of abuses and usurpations, pursuing invariably the same Object evinces a design to reduce them under absolute Despotism, it is their right, it is their duty, to throw off such Government, and to provide new Guards for their future security.--Such has been the patient sufferance of these Colonies; and such is now the necessity which constrains them to alter their former Systems of Government. The history of the present King of Great Britain is a history of repeated injuries and usurpations, all having in direct object the establishment of an absolute Tyranny over these States. To prove this, let Facts be submitted to a candid world.

He has refused his Assent to Laws, the most wholesome and necessary for the public good.

He has forbidden his Governors to pass Laws of immediate and pressing importance, unless suspended in their operation till his Assent should be obtained; and when so suspended, he has utterly neglected to attend to them.

He has refused to pass other Laws for the accommodation of large districts of people, unless those people would relinquish the right of Representation in the Legislature, a right inestimable to them and formidable to tyrants only.

He has called together legislative bodies at places unusual, uncomfortable, and distant from the depository of their public Records, for the sole purpose of fatiguing them into compliance with his measures.

He has dissolved Representative Houses repeatedly, for opposing with manly firmness his invasions on the rights of the people.

He has refused for a long time, after such dissolutions, to cause others to be elected; whereby the Legislative powers, incapable of Annihilation, have returned to the People at large for their exercise; the State remaining in the mean time exposed to all the dangers of invasion from without, and convulsions within.

He has endeavoured to prevent the population of these States; for that purpose obstructing the Laws for Naturalization of Foreigners; refusing to pass others to encourage their migrations hither, and raising the conditions of new Appropriations of Lands.

He has obstructed the Administration of Justice, by refusing his Assent to Laws for establishing Judiciary powers.

He has made Judges dependent on his Will alone, for the tenure of their offices, and the amount and payment of their salaries.

He has erected a multitude of New Offices, and sent hither swarms of Officers to harrass our people, and eat out their substance.

He has kept among us, in times of peace, Standing Armies without the Consent of our legislatures.

He has affected to render the Military independent of and superior to the Civil power.

He has combined with others to subject us to a jurisdiction foreign to our constitution, and unacknowledged by our laws; giving his Assent to their Acts of pretended Legislation:

For Quartering large bodies of armed troops among us:

For protecting them, by a mock Trial, from punishment for any Murders which they should commit on the Inhabitants of these States:

For cutting off our Trade with all parts of the world:

For imposing Taxes on us without our Consent:

For depriving us in many cases, of the benefits of Trial by Jury:

For transporting us beyond Seas to be tried for pretended offences

For abolishing the free System of English Laws in a neighbouring Province, establishing therein an Arbitrary government, and enlarging its Boundaries so as to render it at once an example and fit instrument for introducing the same absolute rule into these Colonies:

For taking away our Charters, abolishing our most valuable Laws, and altering fundamentally the Forms of our Governments:

For suspending our own Legislatures, and declaring themselves invested with power to legislate for us in all cases whatsoever.

He has abdicated Government here, by declaring us out of his Protection and waging War against us.

He has plundered our seas, ravaged our Coasts, burnt our towns, and destroyed the lives of our people.

He is at this time transporting large Armies of foreign Mercenaries to compleat the works of death, desolation and tyranny, already begun with circumstances of Cruelty & perfidy scarcely paralleled in the most barbarous ages, and totally unworthy the Head of a civilized nation.

He has constrained our fellow Citizens taken Captive on the high Seas to bear Arms against their Country, to become the executioners of their friends and Brethren, or to fall themselves by their Hands.

He has excited domestic insurrections amongst us, and has endeavoured to bring on the inhabitants of our frontiers, the merciless Indian Savages, whose known rule of warfare, is an undistinguished destruction of all ages, sexes and conditions.

In every stage of these Oppressions We have Petitioned for Redress in the most humble terms: Our repeated Petitions have been answered only by repeated injury.

A Prince whose character is thus marked by every act which may define a Tyrant, is unfit to be the ruler of a free people.

Nor have We been wanting in attentions to our Brittish brethren. We have warned them from time to time of attempts by their legislature to extend an unwarrantable jurisdiction over us. We have reminded them of the circumstances of our emigration and settlement here. We have appealed to their native justice and magnanimity, and we have conjured them by the ties of our common kindred to disavow these usurpations, which, would inevitably interrupt our connections and correspondence. They too have been deaf to the voice of justice and of consanguinity. We must, therefore, acquiesce in the necessity, which denounces our Separation, and hold them, as we hold the rest of mankind, Enemies in War, in Peace Friends.

We, therefore, the Representatives of the united States of America, in General Congress, Assembled, appealing to the Supreme Judge of the world for the rectitude of our intentions, do, in the Name, and by Authority of the good People of these Colonies, solemnly publish and declare, That these United Colonies are, and of Right ought to be Free and Independent States; that they are Absolved from all Allegiance to the British Crown, and that all political connection between them and the State of Great Britain, is and ought to be totally dissolved; and that as Free and Independent States, they have full Power to levy War, conclude Peace, contract Alliances, establish Commerce, and to do all other Acts and Things which Independent States may of right do. And for the support of this Declaration, with a firm reliance on the protection of divine Providence, we mutually pledge to each other our Lives, our Fortunes and our sacred Honor.

Main ideas of Declaration:

1. Natural Rights: The Declaration of Independence asserts that all individuals are endowed with certain inherent rights that cannot be taken away. These rights are often referred to as "unalienable rights" and include life, liberty, and the pursuit of happiness.

2. Equality: The Declaration states that all men are created equal, emphasizing the notion that individuals should be treated with fairness and without discrimination based on factors such as birth or social status. This principle supports the idea of equal opportunity and equal treatment under the law.

3. Government by Consent: According to the Declaration, governments derive their just powers from the consent of the governed. This means that legitimate political authority is established through the agreement and participation of the people. It implies that governments should serve the interests and protect the rights of the people.

4. Purpose of Government: The Declaration of Independence argues that the primary purpose of government is to secure and protect the rights of individuals. Governments are instituted among people to ensure the safety, well-being, and happiness of society as a whole. If a government fails to fulfill this purpose, the people have the right to alter or abolish it and establish a new system.

5. Right to Revolution: The Declaration acknowledges that under certain circumstances, when a government becomes tyrannical and oppressive, the people have the right to revolt and establish a new government that will better protect their rights and interests. This principle reflects the idea that resistance against unjust authority is justified in defense of individual rights and freedom.

6. Grievances Against King George III: The Declaration of Independence lists a series of specific grievances against King George III, outlining the ways in which he violated the rights of the American colonists. These grievances serve to demonstrate the justifications for the American colonies' desire to separate from British rule.

The Declaration of Independence proclaims the fundamental principles of natural rights, equality, government by consent, and the right to revolution. It not only served as a formal declaration of independence from Great Britain but also laid the philosophical groundwork for the establishment of a new nation committed to protecting individual rights and fostering democratic principles.

Articles of Confederation

To all to whom these Presents shall come, we, the undersigned Delegates of the States affixed to our Names send greeting. Whereas the Delegates of the United States of America in Congress assembled did on the fifteenth day of November in the year of our Lord One Thousand Seven Hundred and Seventy seven, and in the Second Year of the Independence of America agree to certain articles of Confederation and perpetual Union between the States of Newhampshire, Massachusetts-bay, Rhodeisland and Providence Plantations, Connecticut, New York, New Jersey, Pennsylvania, Delaware, Maryland, Virginia, North Carolina, South Carolina, and Georgia in the Words following, viz. "Articles of Confederation and perpetual Union between the States of Newhampshire, Massachusetts-bay, Rhodeisland and Providence Plantations, Connecticut, New York, New Jersey, Pennsylvania, Delaware, Maryland, Virginia, North Carolina, South Carolina, and Georgia.

Article I. The Stile of this confederacy shall be, "The United States of America."

Article II. Each state retains its sovereignty, freedom and independence, and every Power, Jurisdiction and right, which is not by this confederation expressly delegated to the United States, in Congress assembled.

Article III. The said states hereby severally enter into a firm league of friendship with each other, for their common defence, the security of their Liberties, and their mutual and general welfare, binding themselves to assist each other, against all force offered to, or attacks made upon them, or any of them, on account of religion, sovereignty, trade, or any other pretence whatever.

Article IV. The better to secure and perpetuate mutual friendship and intercourse among the people of the different states in this union, the free inhabitants of each of these states, paupers, vagabonds and fugitives from Justice excepted, shall be entitled to all privileges and immunities of free citizens in the several states; and the people of each state shall have free ingress and regress to and from any other state, and shall enjoy therein all the privileges of trade and commerce, subject to the same duties, impositions and restrictions as the inhabitants thereof respectively, provided that such restrictions shall not extend so far as to prevent the removal of property imported into any state, to any other State of which the Owner is an inhabitant; provided also that no imposition, duties or restriction shall be laid by any state, on the property of the united states, or either of them.

If any Person guilty of, or charged with, treason, felony, or other high misdemeanor in any state, shall flee from Justice, and be found in any of the united states, he shall upon demand of the Governor or executive power of the state from which he fled, be delivered up, and removed to the state having jurisdiction of his offence.

Full faith and credit shall be given in each of these states to the records, acts and judicial proceedings of the courts and magistrates of every other state.

Article V. For the more convenient management of the general interests of the united states, delegates shall be annually appointed in such manner as the legislature of each state shall direct, to meet in Congress on the first Monday in November, in every year, with a power reserved to each state to recall its delegates, or any of them, at any time within the year, and to send others in their stead, for the remainder of the Year.

No State shall be represented in Congress by less than two, nor by more than seven Members; and no person shall be capable of being delegate for more than three years, in any term of six years; nor shall any person, being a delegate, be capable of holding any office under the united states, for which he, or another for his benefit receives any salary, fees or emolument of any kind.

Each State shall maintain its own delegates in a meeting of the states, and while they act as members of the committee of the states.

In determining questions in the united states, in Congress assembled, each state shall have one vote.

Freedom of speech and debate in Congress shall not be impeached or questioned in any Court, or place out of Congress, and the members of congress shall be protected in their persons from arrests and imprisonments, during the time of their going to and from, and attendance on congress, except for treason, felony, or breach of the peace.

Article VI. No State, without the Consent of the united States, in congress assembled, shall send any embassy to, or receive any embassy from, or enter into any conferrence, agreement, alliance, or treaty, with any King prince or state; nor shall any person holding any office of profit or trust under the united states, or any of them, accept of any present, emolument, office, or title of any kind whatever, from any king, prince, or foreign state; nor shall the united states, in congress assembled, or any of them, grant any title of nobility.

No two or more states shall enter into any treaty, confederation, or alliance whatever between them, without the consent of the united states, in congress assembled, specifying accurately the purposes for which the same is to be entered into, and how long it shall continue.

No State shall lay any imposts or duties, which may interfere with any stipulations in treaties, entered into by the united States in congress assembled, with any king, prince, or State, in pursuance of any treaties already proposed by congress, to the courts of France and Spain.

No vessels of war shall be kept up in time of peace, by any state, except such number only, as shall be deemed necessary by the united states, in congress assembled, for the defence of such state, or its trade; nor shall any body of forces be kept up, by any state, in time of peace, except such number only as, in the judgment of the united states, in congress assembled, shall be deemed requisite to garrison the forts necessary for the defence of such state; but every state shall always keep up a well regulated and disciplined militia, sufficiently armed and accoutred, and shall provide and constantly have ready for use, in public stores, a due number of field pieces and tents, and a proper quantity of arms, ammunition, and camp equipage.

No State shall engage in any war without the consent of the united States in congress assembled, unless such State be actually invaded by enemies, or shall have received certain advice of a resolution being formed by some nation of Indians to invade such State, and the danger is so imminent as not to admit of a delay till the united states in congress assembled, can be consulted: nor shall any state grant commissions to any ships or vessels of war, nor letters of marque or reprisal, except it be after a declaration of war by the united states in congress assembled, and then only against the kingdom or State, and the subjects thereof, against which war has been so declared, and under such regulations as shall be established by the united states in congress assembled, unless such state be infested by pirates, in which case vessels of war may be fitted out for that occasion, and kept so long as the danger shall continue, or until the united states in congress assembled shall determine otherwise.

Article VII. When land forces are raised by any state, for the common defence, all officers of or under the rank of colonel, shall be appointed by the legislature of each state respectively by whom such forces shall be raised, or in such manner as such state shall direct, and all vacancies shall be filled up by the state which first made appointment.

Article VIII. All charges of war, and all other expenses that shall be incurred for the common defence or general welfare, and allowed by the united states in congress assembled, shall be defrayed out of a common treasury, which shall be supplied by the several states, in proportion to the value of all land within each state, granted to or surveyed for any Person, as such land and the buildings and improvements thereon shall be estimated, according to such mode as the united states, in congress assembled, shall, from time to time, direct and appoint. The taxes for paying that proportion shall be laid and levied by the authority and direction of the legislatures of the several states within the time agreed upon by the united states in congress assembled.

Article IX. The united states, in congress assembled, shall have the sole and exclusive right and power of determining on peace and war, except in the cases mentioned in the sixth article - of sending and receiving ambassadors - entering into treaties and alliances, provided that no treaty of commerce shall be made, whereby the legislative power of the respective states shall be restrained from imposing such imposts and duties on foreigners, as their own people are subjected to, or from prohibiting the exportation or importation of any species of goods or commodities whatsoever - of establishing rules for deciding, in all cases, what captures on land or water shall be legal, and in what manner prizes taken by land or naval forces in the service of the united Sates, shall be divided or appropriated - of granting letters of marque and reprisal in times of peace - appointing courts for the trial of piracies and felonies committed on the high seas; and establishing courts; for receiving and determining finally appeals in all cases of captures; provided that no member of congress shall be appointed a judge of any of the said courts.

The united states, in congress assembled, shall also be the last resort on appeal, in all disputes and differences now subsisting, or that hereafter may arise between two or more states concerning boundary, jurisdiction, or any other cause whatever; which authority shall always be exercised in the manner following. Whenever the legislative or executive authority, or lawful agent of any state in controversy with another, shall present a petition to congress, stating the matter in question, and praying for a hearing, notice thereof shall be given, by order of congress, to the legislative or executive authority of the other state in controversy, and a day assigned for the appearance of the parties by their lawful agents, who shall then be directed to appoint, by joint consent, commissioners or judges to constitute a court for hearing and determining the matter in question: but if they cannot agree, congress shall name three persons out of each of the united states, and from the list of such persons each party shall alternately strike out one, the petitioners beginning, until the number shall be reduced to thirteen; and from that number not less than seven, nor more than nine names, as congress shall direct, shall, in the presence of congress, be drawn out by lot, and the persons whose names shall be so drawn, or any five of them, shall be commissioners or judges, to hear and finally determine the controversy, so always as a major part of the judges, who shall hear the cause, shall agree in the determination: and if either party shall neglect to attend at the day appointed, without showing reasons which congress shall judge sufficient, or being present, shall refuse to strike, the congress shall proceed to nominate three persons out of each State, and the secretary of congress shall strike in behalf of such party absent or refusing; and the judgment and sentence of the court, to be appointed in the manner before prescribed, shall be final and conclusive; and if any of the parties shall refuse to submit to the authority of such court, or to appear or defend their claim or cause, the court shall nevertheless proceed to pronounce sentence, or judgment, which shall in like manner be final and decisive; the judgment or sentence and other proceedings being in either case transmitted to congress, and lodged among the acts of congress, for the security of the parties concerned: provided that every commissioner, before he sits in judgment, shall take an oath to be administered by one of the judges of the supreme or superior court of the State where the cause shall be tried, "well and truly to hear and determine the matter in question, according to the best of his judgment, without favour, affection, or hope of reward: "provided, also, that no State shall be deprived of territory for the benefit of the united states.

All controversies concerning the private right of soil claimed under different grants of two or more states, whose jurisdictions as they may respect such lands, and the states which passed such grants are adjusted, the said grants or either of them being at the same time claimed to have originated antecedent to such settlement of jurisdiction, shall, on the petition of either party to the congress of the united states, be finally determined, as near as may be, in the same manner as is before prescribed for deciding disputes respecting territorial jurisdiction between different states.

The united states, in congress assembled, shall also have the sole and exclusive right and power of regulating the alloy and value of coin struck by their own authority, or by that of the respective states - fixing the standard of weights and measures throughout the united states - regulating the trade and managing all affairs with the Indians, not members of any of the states; provided that the legislative right of any state, within its own limits, be not infringed or violated - establishing and regulating post-offices from one state to another, throughout all the united states, and exacting such postage on the papers passing through the same, as may be requisite to defray the expenses of the said office - appointing all officers of the land forces in the service of the united States, excepting regimental officers - appointing all the officers of the naval forces, and commissioning all officers whatever in the service of the united states; making rules for the government and regulation of the said land and naval forces, and directing their operations.

The united States, in congress assembled, shall have authority to appoint a committee, to sit in the recess of congress, to be denominated, "A Committee of the States," and to consist of one delegate from each State; and to appoint such other committees and civil officers as may be necessary for managing the general affairs of the united states under their direction - to appoint one of their number to preside; provided that no person be allowed to serve in the office of president more than one year in any term of three years; to ascertain the necessary sums of money to be raised for the service of the united states, and to appropriate and apply the same for defraying the public expenses; to borrow money or emit bills on the credit of the united states, transmitting every half year to the respective states an account of the sums of money so borrowed or emitted, - to build and equip a navy - to agree upon the number of land forces, and to make requisitions from each state for its quota, in proportion to the number of white inhabitants in such state, which requisition shall be binding; and thereupon the legislature of each state shall appoint the regimental officers, raise the men, and clothe, arm, and equip them, in a soldier-like manner, at the expense of the united states; and the officers and men so clothed, armed, and equipped, shall march to the place appointed, and within the time agreed on by the united states, in congress assembled; but if the united states, in congress assembled, shall, on consideration of circumstances, judge proper that any state should not raise men, or should raise a smaller number than its quota, and that any other state should raise a greater number of men than the quota thereof, such extra number shall be raised, officered, clothed, armed, and equipped in the same manner as the quota of such state, unless the legislature of such state shall judge that such extra number cannot be safely spared out of the same, in which case they shall raise, officer, clothe, arm, and equip, as many of such extra number as they judge can be safely spared. And the officers and men so clothed, armed, and equipped, shall march to the place appointed, and within the time agreed on by the united states in congress assembled.

The united states, in congress assembled, shall never engage in a war, nor grant letters of marque and reprisal in time of peace, nor enter into any treaties or alliances, nor coin money, nor regulate the value thereof nor ascertain the sums and expenses necessary for the defence and welfare of the united states, or any of them, nor emit bills, nor borrow money on the credit of the united states, nor appropriate money, nor agree upon the number of vessels of war to be built or purchased, or the number of land or sea forces to be raised, nor appoint a commander in chief of the army or navy, unless nine states assent to the same, nor shall a question on any other point, except for adjourning from day to day, be determined, unless by the votes of a majority of the united states in congress assembled.

The congress of the united states shall have power to adjourn to any time within the year, and to any place within the united states, so that no period of adjournment be for a longer duration than the space of six Months, and shall publish the Journal of their proceedings monthly, except such parts thereof relating to treaties, alliances, or military operations, as in their judgment require secrecy; and the yeas and nays of the delegates of each State, on any question, shall be entered on the Journal, when it is desired by any delegate; and the delegates of a State, or any of them, at his or their request, shall be furnished with a transcript of the said Journal, except such parts as are above excepted, to lay before the legislatures of the several states.

Article X. The committee of the states, or any nine of them, shall be authorized to execute, in the recess of congress, such of the powers of congress as the united states, in congress assembled, by the consent of nine states, shall, from time to time, think expedient to vest them with; provided that no power be delegated to the said committee, for the exercise of which, by the articles of confederation, the voice of nine states, in the congress of the united states assembled, is requisite.

Article XI. Canada acceding to this confederation, and joining in the measures of the united states, shall be admitted into, and entitled to all the advantages of this union: but no other colony shall be admitted into the same, unless such admission be agreed to by nine states.

Article XII. All bills of credit emitted, monies borrowed, and debts contracted by or under the authority of congress, before the assembling of the united states, in pursuance of the present confederation, shall be deemed and considered as a charge against the united States, for payment and satisfaction whereof the said united states and the public faith are hereby solemnly pledged.

Article XIII. Every State shall abide by the determinations of the united states, in congress assembled, on all questions which by this confederation are submitted to them. And the Articles of this confederation shall be inviolably observed by every state, and the union shall be perpetual; nor shall any alteration at any time hereafter be made in any of them, unless such alteration be agreed to in a congress of the united states, and be afterwards con-firmed by the legislatures of every state.

And Whereas it hath pleased the Great Governor of the World to incline the hearts of the legislatures we respectively represent in congress, to approve of, and to authorize us to ratify the said articles of confederation and perpetual union, Know Ye, that we, the undersigned delegates, by virtue of the power and authority to us given for that purpose, do, by these presents, in the name and in behalf of our respective constituents, fully and entirely ratify and confirm each and every of the said articles of confederation and perpetual union, and all and singular the matters and things therein contained. And we do further solemnly plight and engage the faith of our respective constituents, that they shall abide by the determinations of the united states in congress assembled, on all questions, which by the said confederation are submitted to them. And that the articles thereof shall be inviolably observed by the states we respectively represent, and that the union shall be perpetual.

Main points of the Articles:

The Articles of Confederation served as the first constitution of the United States from 1781 to 1789. Here's a summary of its main points:

1. Structure of Government: The Articles of Confederation established a system of government that emphasized a loose alliance among the thirteen original states. The central government was intentionally kept weak, with most powers residing in the individual states.

2. Legislative Branch: The Confederation Congress was the primary governing body under the Articles. Each state had one vote in Congress, and decisions required the approval of a majority of states. However, Congress lacked the power to enforce its laws or collect taxes directly.

3. Powers of Congress: Congress had limited authority, mainly in areas such as declaring war, conducting foreign affairs, and maintaining an army and navy. It could also establish a postal service and settle disputes among the states. However, it lacked the power to regulate commerce or levy taxes.

4. State Sovereignty: The Articles of Confederation aimed to protect the sovereignty of individual states. Each state retained its own laws, currency, and control over internal affairs. The central government had no authority to interfere with the internal governance of the states.

5. Weak Executive: The Articles did not establish an executive branch separate from Congress. Instead, there was a president of Congress, elected by the members, who held limited powers and acted as a presiding officer.

6. Amendment Process: Amending the Articles required the unanimous consent of all thirteen states, making it difficult to implement changes or address flaws in the system.

7. Weak Central Authority: One of the main weaknesses of the Articles of Confederation was the lack of a strong central authority. The central government had limited powers and struggled to coordinate actions or enforce its decisions effectively.

8. Financial Issues: The central government could not levy taxes directly, relying on voluntary contributions from the states. This often led to financial instability and an inability to pay off debts incurred during the Revolutionary War.

9. Limited Regulation of Trade: The central government lacked the power to regulate trade between states or with foreign nations, leading to economic disputes and barriers to interstate commerce.

10. Challenges and Reforms: The shortcomings of the Articles of Confederation, including financial instability, weak central authority, and difficulties in governing, eventually led to the call for a stronger national government, resulting in the drafting of the U.S. Constitution.

Overall, the Articles of Confederation emphasized state sovereignty, a weak central government, and limited powers for Congress. Its shortcomings highlighted the need for a more robust and cohesive federal system, which led to the eventual replacement of the Articles with the U.S. Constitution.

As an introduction to the Constitution, contrast it with the Articles:

1. Structure of Government:
   - Articles of Confederation: The government structure under the Articles was characterized by a weak central government, where power was primarily held by the states. There was no separate executive branch, and Congress served as the main governing body.
   - Constitution: The Constitution established a stronger central government with a system of checks and balances. It created separate branches—executive, legislative, and judicial—with defined powers and responsibilities.

2. Powers of the Central Government:
   - Articles of Confederation: The central government had limited powers, primarily including the ability to conduct foreign affairs, declare war, and manage disputes between states. It lacked the power to levy taxes, regulate commerce, or enforce its laws effectively.
   - Constitution: The Constitution granted the central government more extensive powers, such as the authority to levy taxes, regulate interstate commerce, and establish a national defense. It provided for a stronger federal presence in governance.

3. Representation:
   - Articles of Confederation: Each state had one vote in Congress, regardless of size or population. This equal representation meant that smaller states had an equal voice to larger states.
   - Constitution: The Constitution established a bicameral legislature, with representation in the House of Representatives based on population and equal representation in the Senate, where each state has two senators.

4. Amendment Process:
   - Articles of Confederation: Amending the Articles required unanimous consent from all thirteen states, making it difficult to enact changes.
   - Constitution: The Constitution created a more flexible amendment process. Amendments can be proposed by Congress or through a constitutional convention, and ratification requires the approval of three-fourths of the states.

5. Executive Branch:
   - Articles of Confederation: The central government had no separate executive branch. The president of Congress served as a presiding officer with limited powers.

- Constitution: The Constitution established a separate executive branch headed by the President, with powers to enforce laws, make executive decisions, and serve as the head of state.

6. Judicial System:
   - Articles of Confederation: The central government had no established federal court system.
   - Constitution: The Constitution created a federal judiciary, including the Supreme Court, to interpret laws, resolve disputes, and ensure the constitutionality of legislation.

7. Supremacy Clause:
   - Articles of Confederation: The states retained significant sovereignty, and the central government had limited authority over them.
   - Constitution: The Supremacy Clause in the Constitution established federal law as the supreme law of the land, giving the central government greater authority over the states.

8. Military/Standing Army:
   -Articles of Confederation: The central government under the Articles had difficulty maintaining a standing army. It relied heavily on requisitions from the states for troops and supplies during times of war.
   -Constitution: The Constitution addressed the weaknesses of the military under the Articles by granting the central government the power to maintain a standing army. Congress was responsible for raising and supporting the military forces, and the President had command over the military as the Commander-in-Chief.

Overall, the Constitution established a stronger central government, provided for a system of checks and balances, expanded the powers of the federal government, and addressed the shortcomings of the Articles of Confederation. It aimed to create a more stable, unified, and effective system of governance for the United States.

The Constitution

We the People of the United States, in Order to form a more perfect Union, establish Justice, insure domestic Tranquility, provide for the common defence, promote the general Welfare, and secure the Blessings of Liberty to ourselves and our Posterity, do ordain and establish this Constitution for the United States of America.

Article I
Section 1
All legislative Powers herein granted shall be vested in a Congress of the United States, which shall consist of a Senate and House of Representatives.

Section 2
The House of Representatives shall be composed of Members chosen every second Year by the People of the several States, and the Electors in each State shall have the Qualifications requisite for Electors of the most numerous Branch of the State Legislature.

No Person shall be a Representative who shall not have attained to the Age of twenty five Years, and been seven Years a Citizen of the United States, and who shall not, when elected, be an Inhabitant of that State in which he shall be chosen.

Representatives and direct Taxes shall be apportioned among the several States which may be included within this Union, according to their respective Numbers, which shall be determined by adding to the whole Number of free Persons, including those bound to Service for a Term of Years, and excluding Indians not taxed, three fifths of all other Persons. The actual Enumeration shall be made within three Years after the first Meeting of the Congress of the United States, and within every subsequent Term of ten Years, in such Manner as they shall by Law direct. The Number of Representatives shall not exceed one for every thirty Thousand, but each State shall have at Least one Representative; and until such enumeration shall be made, the State of New Hampshire shall be entitled to chuse three, Massachusetts eight, Rhode-Island and Providence Plantations one, Connecticut five, New-York six, New Jersey four, Pennsylvania eight, Delaware one, Maryland six, Virginia ten, North Carolina five, South Carolina five, and Georgia three.

When vacancies happen in the Representation from any State, the Executive Authority thereof shall issue Writs of Election to fill such Vacancies.

The House of Representatives shall chuse their Speaker and other Officers; and shall have the sole Power of Impeachment.

Section 3

The Senate of the United States shall be composed of two Senators from each State, chosen by the Legislature thereof, for six Years; and each Senator shall have one Vote.

Immediately after they shall be assembled in Consequence of the first Election, they shall be divided as equally as may be into three Classes. The Seats of the Senators of the first Class shall be vacated at the Expiration of the second Year, of the second Class at the Expiration of the fourth Year, and of the third Class at the Expiration of the sixth Year, so that one third may be chosen every second Year; and if Vacancies happen by Resignation, or otherwise, during the Recess of the Legislature of any State, the Executive thereof may make temporary Appointments until the next Meeting of the Legislature, which shall then fill such Vacancies.

No Person shall be a Senator who shall not have attained to the Age of thirty Years, and been nine Years a Citizen of the United States, and who shall not, when elected, be an Inhabitant of that State for which he shall be chosen.

The Vice President of the United States shall be President of the Senate, but shall have no Vote, unless they be equally divided.

The Senate shall chuse their other Officers, and also a President pro tempore, in the Absence of the Vice President, or when he shall exercise the Office of President of the United States.

The Senate shall have the sole Power to try all Impeachments. When sitting for that Purpose, they shall be on Oath or Affirmation. When the President of the United States is tried, the Chief Justice shall preside: And no Person shall be convicted without the Concurrence of two thirds of the Members present.

Judgment in Cases of Impeachment shall not extend further than to removal from Office, and disqualification to hold and enjoy any Office of honor, Trust or Profit under the United States: but the Party convicted shall nevertheless be liable and subject to Indictment, Trial, Judgment and Punishment, according to Law.

Section 4

The Times, Places and Manner of holding Elections for Senators and Representatives, shall be prescribed in each State by the Legislature thereof; but the Congress may at any time by Law make or alter such Regulations, except as to the Places of chusing Senators.

The Congress shall assemble at least once in every Year, and such Meeting shall be on the first Monday in December, unless they shall by Law appoint a different Day.

Section 5

Each House shall be the Judge of the Elections, Returns and Qualifications of its own Members, and a Majority of each shall constitute a Quorum to do Business; but a smaller Number may adjourn from day to day, and may be authorized to compel the Attendance of absent Members, in such Manner, and under such Penalties as each House may provide.

Each House may determine the Rules of its Proceedings, punish its Members for disorderly Behaviour, and, with the Concurrence of two thirds, expel a Member.

Each House shall keep a Journal of its Proceedings, and from time to time publish the same, excepting such Parts as may in their Judgment require Secrecy; and the Yeas and Nays of the Members of either House on any question shall, at the Desire of one fifth of those Present, be entered on the Journal.

Neither House, during the Session of Congress, shall, without the Consent of the other, adjourn for more than three days, nor to any other Place than that in which the two Houses shall be sitting.

Section 6

The Senators and Representatives shall receive a Compensation for their Services, to be ascertained by Law, and paid out of the Treasury of the United States. They shall in all Cases, except Treason, Felony and Breach of the Peace, be privileged from Arrest during their Attendance at the Session of their respective Houses, and in going to and returning from the same; and for any Speech or Debate in either House, they shall not be questioned in any other Place.

No Senator or Representative shall, during the Time for which he was elected, be appointed to any civil Office under the Authority of the United States, which shall have been created, or the Emoluments whereof shall have been encreased during such time; and no Person holding any Office under the United States, shall be a Member of either House during his Continuance in Office.

Section 7
All Bills for raising Revenue shall originate in the House of Representatives; but the Senate may propose or concur with Amendments as on other Bills.

Every Bill which shall have passed the House of Representatives and the Senate, shall, before it become a Law, be presented to the President of the United States; If he approve he shall sign it, but if not he shall return it, with his Objections to that House in which it shall have originated, who shall enter the Objections at large on their Journal, and proceed to reconsider it. If after such Reconsideration two thirds of that House shall agree to pass the Bill, it shall be sent, together with the Objections, to the other House, by which it shall likewise be reconsidered, and if approved by two thirds of that House, it shall become a Law. But in all such Cases the Votes of both Houses shall be determined by yeas and Nays, and the Names of the Persons voting for and against the Bill shall be entered on the Journal of each House respectively. If any Bill shall not be returned by the President within ten Days (Sundays excepted) after it shall have been presented to him, the Same shall be a Law, in like Manner as if he had signed it, unless the Congress by their Adjournment prevent its Return, in which Case it shall not be a Law.

Every Order, Resolution, or Vote to which the Concurrence of the Senate and House of Representatives may be necessary (except on a question of Adjournment) shall be presented to the President of the United States; and before the Same shall take Effect, shall be approved by him, or being disapproved by him, shall be repassed by two thirds of the Senate and House of Representatives, according to the Rules and Limitations prescribed in the Case of a Bill.

Section 8
The Congress shall have Power To lay and collect Taxes, Duties, Imposts and Excises, to pay the Debts and provide for the common Defence and general Welfare of the United States; but all Duties, Imposts and Excises shall be uniform throughout the United States;

To borrow Money on the credit of the United States;

To regulate Commerce with foreign Nations, and among the several States, and with the Indian Tribes;

To establish an uniform Rule of Naturalization, and uniform Laws on the subject of Bankruptcies throughout the United States;

To coin Money, regulate the Value thereof, and of foreign Coin, and fix the Standard of Weights and Measures;

To provide for the Punishment of counterfeiting the Securities and current Coin of the United States;

To establish Post Offices and post Roads;

To promote the Progress of Science and useful Arts, by securing for limited Times to Authors and Inventors the exclusive Right to their respective Writings and Discoveries;

To constitute Tribunals inferior to the supreme Court;

To define and punish Piracies and Felonies committed on the high Seas, and Offences against the Law of Nations;

To declare War, grant Letters of Marque and Reprisal, and make Rules concerning Captures on Land and Water;

To raise and support Armies, but no Appropriation of Money to that Use shall be for a longer Term than two Years;

To provide and maintain a Navy;

To make Rules for the Government and Regulation of the land and naval Forces;

To provide for calling forth the Militia to execute the Laws of the Union, suppress Insurrections and repel Invasions;

To provide for organizing, arming, and disciplining, the Militia, and for governing such Part of them as may be employed in the Service of the United States, reserving to the States respectively, the Appointment of the Officers, and the Authority of training the Militia according to the discipline prescribed by Congress;

To exercise exclusive Legislation in all Cases whatsoever, over such District (not exceeding ten Miles square) as may, by Cession of particular States, and the Acceptance of Congress, become the Seat of the Government of the United States, and to exercise like Authority over all Places purchased by the Consent of the Legislature of the State in which the Same shall be, for the Erection of Forts, Magazines, Arsenals, dock-Yards, and other needful Buildings;—And

To make all Laws which shall be necessary and proper for carrying into Execution the foregoing Powers, and all other Powers vested by this Constitution in the Government of the United States, or in any Department or Officer thereof.

Section 9

The Migration or Importation of such Persons as any of the States now existing shall think proper to admit, shall not be prohibited by the Congress prior to the Year one thousand eight hundred and eight, but a Tax or duty may be imposed on such Importation, not exceeding ten dollars for each Person.

The Privilege of the Writ of Habeas Corpus shall not be suspended, unless when in Cases of Rebellion or Invasion the public Safety may require it.

No Bill of Attainder or ex post facto Law shall be passed.

No Capitation, or other direct, Tax shall be laid, unless in Proportion to the Census or enumeration herein before directed to be taken.

No Tax or Duty shall be laid on Articles exported from any State.

No Preference shall be given by any Regulation of Commerce or Revenue to the Ports of one State over those of another: nor shall Vessels bound to, or from, one State, be obliged to enter, clear, or pay Duties in another.

No Money shall be drawn from the Treasury, but in Consequence of Appropriations made by Law; and a regular Statement and Account of the Receipts and Expenditures of all public Money shall be published from time to time.

No Title of Nobility shall be granted by the United States: And no Person holding any Office of Profit or Trust under them, shall, without the Consent of the Congress, accept of any present, Emolument, Office, or Title, of any kind whatever, from any King, Prince, or foreign State.

Section 10

No State shall enter into any Treaty, Alliance, or Confederation; grant Letters of Marque and Reprisal; coin Money; emit Bills of Credit; make any Thing but gold and silver Coin a Tender in Payment of Debts; pass any Bill of Attainder, ex post facto Law, or Law impairing the Obligation of Contracts, or grant any Title of Nobility.

No State shall, without the Consent of the Congress, lay any Imposts or Duties on Imports or Exports, except what may be absolutely necessary for executing it's inspection Laws: and the net Produce of all Duties and Imposts, laid by any State on Imports or Exports, shall be for the Use of the Treasury of the United States; and all such Laws shall be subject to the Revision and Control of the Congress.

No State shall, without the Consent of Congress, lay any Duty of Tonnage, keep Troops, or Ships of War in time of Peace, enter into any Agreement or Compact with another State, or with a foreign Power, or engage in War, unless actually invaded, or in such imminent Danger as will not admit of delay.

Article 2

Section 1

The executive Power shall be vested in a President of the United States of America. He shall hold his Office during the Term of four Years, and, together with the Vice President, chosen for the same Term, be elected, as follows

Each State shall appoint, in such Manner as the Legislature thereof may direct, a Number of Electors, equal to the whole Number of Senators and Representatives to which the State may be entitled in the Congress: but no Senator or Representative, or Person holding an Office of Trust or Profit under the United States, shall be appointed an Elector.

The Electors shall meet in their respective States, and vote by Ballot for two Persons, of whom one at least shall not be an Inhabitant of the same State with themselves. And they shall make a List of all the Persons voted for, and of the Number of Votes for each; which List they shall sign and certify, and transmit sealed to the Seat of the Government of the United States, directed to the President of the Senate. The President of the Senate shall, in the Presence of the Senate and House of Representatives, open all the Certificates, and the Votes shall then be counted. The Person having the greatest Number of Votes shall be the President, if such Number be a Majority of the whole Number of Electors appointed; and if there be more than one who have such Majority, and have an equal Number of Votes, then the House of Representatives shall immediately chuse by Ballot one of them for President; and if no Person have a Majority, then from the five highest on the List the said House shall in like Manner chuse the President. But in chusing the President, the Votes shall be taken by States, the Representation from each State having one Vote; A quorum for this Purpose shall consist of a Member or Members from two thirds of the States, and a Majority of all the States shall be necessary to a Choice. In every Case, after the Choice of the President, the Person having the greatest Number of Votes of the Electors shall be the Vice President. But if there should remain two or more who have equal Votes, the Senate shall chuse from them by Ballot the Vice President.

The Congress may determine the Time of chusing the Electors, and the Day on which they shall give their Votes; which Day shall be the same throughout the United States.

No Person except a natural born Citizen, or a Citizen of the United States, at the time of the Adoption of this Constitution, shall be eligible to the Office of President; neither shall any Person be eligible to that Office who shall not have attained to the

Age of thirty five Years, and been fourteen Years a Resident within the United States.

In Case of the Removal of the President from Office, or of his Death, Resignation, or Inability to discharge the Powers and Duties of the said Office, the Same shall devolve on the Vice President, and the Congress may by Law provide for the Case of Removal, Death, Resignation or Inability, both of the President and Vice President, declaring what Officer shall then act as President, and such Officer shall act accordingly, until the Disability be removed, or a President shall be elected.

The President shall, at stated Times, receive for his Services, a Compensation, which shall neither be encreased nor diminished during the Period for which he shall have been elected, and he shall not receive within that Period any other Emolument from the United States, or any of them.

Before he enter on the Execution of his Office, he shall take the following Oath or Affirmation:—"I do solemnly swear (or affirm) that I will faithfully execute the Office of President of the United States, and will to the best of my Ability, preserve, protect and defend the Constitution of the United States."

Section 2

The President shall be Commander in Chief of the Army and Navy of the United States, and of the Militia of the several States, when called into the actual Service of the United States; he may require the Opinion, in writing, of the principal Officer in each of the executive Departments, upon any Subject relating to the Duties of their respective Offices, and he shall have Power to grant Reprieves and Pardons for Offences against the United States, except in Cases of Impeachment.

He shall have Power, by and with the Advice and Consent of the Senate, to make Treaties, provided two thirds of the Senators present concur; and he shall nominate, and by and with the Advice and Consent of the Senate, shall appoint Ambassadors, other public Ministers and Consuls, Judges of the supreme Court, and all other Officers of the United States, whose Appointments are not herein otherwise provided for, and which shall be established by Law: but the Congress may by Law vest the Appointment of such inferior Officers, as they think proper, in the President alone, in the Courts of Law, or in the Heads of Departments.

The President shall have Power to fill up all Vacancies that may happen during the Recess of the Senate, by granting Commissions which shall expire at the End of their next Session.

Section 3

He shall from time to time give to the Congress Information of the State of the Union, and recommend to their Consideration such Measures as he shall judge necessary and expedient; he may, on extraordinary Occasions, convene both Houses, or either of them, and in Case of Disagreement between them, with Respect to the Time of Adjournment, he may adjourn them to such Time as he shall think proper; he shall receive Ambassadors and other public Ministers; he shall take Care that the Laws be faithfully executed, and shall Commission all the Officers of the United States.

Section 4
The President, Vice President and all civil Officers of the United States, shall be removed from Office on Impeachment for, and Conviction of, Treason, Bribery, or other high Crimes and Misdemeanors.

Article 3
Section 1
The judicial Power of the United States, shall be vested in one supreme Court, and in such inferior Courts as the Congress may from time to time ordain and establish. The Judges, both of the supreme and inferior Courts, shall hold their Offices during good Behaviour, and shall, at stated Times, receive for their Services, a Compensation, which shall not be diminished during their Continuance in Office.

Section 2
The judicial Power shall extend to all Cases, in Law and Equity, arising under this Constitution, the Laws of the United States, and Treaties made, or which shall be made, under their Authority;—to all Cases affecting Ambassadors, other public Ministers and Consuls;—to all Cases of admiralty and maritime Jurisdiction;—to Controversies to which the United States shall be a Party;—to Controversies between two or more States;— between a State and Citizens of another State,—between Citizens of different States,—between Citizens of the same State claiming Lands under Grants of different States, and between a State, or the Citizens thereof, and foreign States, Citizens or Subjects.

In all Cases affecting Ambassadors, other public Ministers and Consuls, and those in which a State shall be Party, the supreme Court shall have original Jurisdiction. In all the other Cases before mentioned, the supreme Court shall have appellate Jurisdiction, both as to Law and Fact, with such Exceptions, and under such Regulations as the Congress shall make.

The Trial of all Crimes, except in Cases of Impeachment, shall be by Jury; and such Trial shall be held in the State where the said Crimes shall have been committed; but when not committed within any State, the Trial shall be at such Place or Places as the Congress may by Law have directed.

Section 3

Treason against the United States, shall consist only in levying War against them, or in adhering to their Enemies, giving them Aid and Comfort. No Person shall be convicted of Treason unless on the Testimony of two Witnesses to the same overt Act, or on Confession in open Court.

The Congress shall have Power to declare the Punishment of Treason, but no Attainder of Treason shall work Corruption of Blood, or Forfeiture except during the Life of the Person attainted.

Article 4

Section 1

Full Faith and Credit shall be given in each State to the public Acts, Records, and judicial Proceedings of every other State. And the Congress may by general Laws prescribe the Manner in which such Acts, Records and Proceedings shall be proved, and the Effect thereof.

Section 2

The Citizens of each State shall be entitled to all Privileges and Immunities of Citizens in the several States.

A Person charged in any State with Treason, Felony, or other Crime, who shall flee from Justice, and be found in another State, shall on Demand of the executive Authority of the State from which he fled, be delivered up, to be removed to the State having Jurisdiction of the Crime.

No Person held to Service or Labour in one State, under the Laws thereof, escaping into another, shall, in Consequence of any Law or Regulation therein, be discharged from such Service or Labour, but shall be delivered up on Claim of the Party to whom such Service or Labour may be due.

Section 3

New States may be admitted by the Congress into this Union; but no new State shall be formed or erected within the Jurisdiction of any other State; nor any State be formed by the Junction of two or more States, or Parts of States, without the Consent of the Legislatures of the States concerned as well as of the Congress.

The Congress shall have Power to dispose of and make all needful Rules and Regulations respecting the Territory or other Property belonging to the United States; and nothing in this Constitution shall be so construed as to Prejudice any Claims of the United States, or of any particular State.

Section 4

The United States shall guarantee to every State in this Union a Republican Form of Government, and shall protect each of them against Invasion; and on Application of the Legislature, or of the Executive (when the Legislature cannot be convened) against domestic Violence.

Article 5

The Congress, whenever two thirds of both Houses shall deem it necessary, shall propose Amendments to this Constitution, or, on the Application of the Legislatures of two thirds of the several States, shall call a Convention for proposing Amendments, which, in either Case, shall be valid to all Intents and Purposes, as Part of this Constitution, when ratified by the Legislatures of three fourths of the several States, or by Conventions in three fourths thereof, as the one or the other Mode of Ratification may be proposed by the Congress; Provided that no Amendment which may be made prior to the Year One thousand eight hundred and eight shall in any Manner affect the first and fourth Clauses in the Ninth Section of the first Article; and that no State, without its Consent, shall be deprived of its equal Suffrage in the Senate.

Article 6

All Debts contracted and Engagements entered into, before the Adoption of this Constitution, shall be as valid against the United States under this Constitution, as under the Confederation.

This Constitution, and the Laws of the United States which shall be made in Pursuance thereof; and all Treaties made, or which shall be made, under the Authority of the United States, shall be the supreme Law of the Land; and the Judges in every State shall be bound thereby, any Thing in the Constitution or Laws of any State to the Contrary notwithstanding.

The Senators and Representatives before mentioned, and the Members of the several State Legislatures, and all executive and judicial Officers, both of the United States and of the several States, shall be bound by Oath or Affirmation, to support this Constitution; but no religious Test shall ever be required as a Qualification to any Office or public Trust under the United States.

Article 7

The Ratification of the Conventions of nine States, shall be sufficient for the Establishment of this Constitution between the States so ratifying the Same.

Summary of main provisions of the Constitution

Article 1: Legislative Branch

- Section 1: Establishes the bicameral Congress, consisting of the House of Representatives and the Senate.

- Section 2: Defines the composition, qualifications, and powers of the House of Representatives.

- Section 3: Defines the composition, qualifications, and powers of the Senate.

- Section 4: Addresses the time, place, and manner of holding congressional elections.

- Section 5: Specifies the rules, procedures, and requirements for the operation of Congress.

- Section 6: Outlines the privileges and restrictions for members of Congress.

- Section 7: Establishes the process for passing bills and the requirement for presidential approval or veto.

- Section 8: Enumerates the specific powers of Congress, including taxation, defense, and commerce regulation.

The United States Constitution grants specific powers to the federal government, known as enumerated powers. These powers are outlined in Article I, Section 8 of the Constitution. Here is a list of the enumerated powers along with brief explanations:

1. Power to Tax and Spend: Congress has the authority to levy taxes, collect revenue, and allocate public funds for the functioning of the government and the provision of public services.

2. Power to **Regulate Commerce:** Congress can regulate interstate and foreign commerce, which includes trade and economic activities that cross state or national boundaries[2].

3. Power to Coin Money and Regulate Currency: The federal government has the exclusive authority to create and regulate the country's currency, including the power to coin money and set standards for its value.

4. Power to Establish Post Offices and Roads: Congress can establish post offices and postal roads to facilitate communication and transportation across the country.

5. Power to Declare War: Only Congress has the authority to declare war, determining when the nation engages in armed conflict.

6. Power to Raise and Support an Army and Navy: Congress can raise and maintain a military force, including the power to draft troops, provide for their training and equipment, and maintain a navy.

7. Power to Establish Courts: The federal government can establish and maintain the federal court system, including the Supreme Court, and define the jurisdiction and structure of these courts.

8. Power to Grant Patents and Copyrights: Congress can issue patents and copyrights to protect the rights of inventors and authors, encouraging innovation and creativity.

9. Power to Establish Naturalization Laws: The federal government has the authority to establish rules and procedures for the naturalization of immigrants, granting them citizenship.

10. **Power to Make Laws Necessary and Proper:** Also known as the "Elastic Clause" or the "Necessary and Proper Clause," this power allows Congress to

---

[2] The Commerce Clause is a provision in Article I, Section 8, Clause 3 of the United States Constitution. It grants Congress the power to regulate commerce among the states, with foreign nations, and with Native American tribes. The interpretation and expansiveness of the Commerce Clause have been subjects of considerable debate and controversy throughout American history. The Commerce Clause was included in the Constitution to address the need for a unified economic system among the states and to prevent trade barriers and economic disputes that plagued the nation under the Articles of Confederation. At the time of its drafting, the primary concern was to eliminate trade barriers and ensure a free flow of commerce between the states. Over the years, the interpretation of the Commerce Clause has expanded, and it has become a significant source of congressional authority to regulate a wide range of economic activities. The Supreme Court has played a crucial role in shaping the understanding and scope of the Commerce Clause through its interpretations in landmark cases.

make laws that are necessary and proper for executing its other enumerated powers effectively[3].

These enumerated powers grant specific authority to the federal government, while also establishing a system of checks and balances with other branches of government, such as the executive and judicial branches, to ensure a separation of powers and safeguard individual liberties.

- Section 9: Imposes limitations on the powers of Congress, such as prohibiting the suspension of habeas corpus[4] and passing bills of attainder[5].

- Section 10: Places limitations on the powers of the states, such as entering into treaties or alliances.

Article 2: Executive Branch
- Section 1: Establishes the office of the President and outlines the method of selection and the qualifications for holding the office.

- Section 2: Details the powers and responsibilities of the President, including the role as commander-in-chief of the military and the ability to make treaties and appoint officials.
- Section 3: Outlines the President's duty to give Congress information and recommends measures.

- Section 4: Addresses the impeachment and removal of the President for high crimes and misdemeanors.

----

[3] The Necessary and Proper Clause, also known as the "Elastic Clause" or the "Implied Powers Clause," is found in Article I, Section 8, Clause 18 of the United States Constitution. It states that Congress has the power to make all laws which shall be necessary and proper for carrying out its other enumerated powers. The meaning and expansiveness of the Necessary and Proper Clause have been the subject of interpretation and debate throughout American history. The clause grants Congress the authority to enact laws that are not explicitly listed in the Constitution but are deemed necessary and appropriate to execute the powers granted to the federal government. This provision expands the scope of congressional authority beyond the specifically enumerated powers, allowing Congress to address unforeseen circumstances and adapt to changing societal needs. The Necessary and Proper Clause has been central to the concept of implied powers, which are powers inferred from the express powers granted in the Constitution. Implied powers are not explicitly stated but are considered necessary to carry out the expressed powers. The clause provides a constitutional basis for Congress to exercise implied powers.
[4] Habeas corpus is a fundamental legal principle that safeguards individual liberty by protecting against arbitrary detention or imprisonment. The term "habeas corpus" is Latin for "you shall have the body." The concept ensures that individuals who are detained have the right to challenge the legality of their detention before a court.
[5] A bill of attainder is a legislative act that declares a specific individual or group guilty of a crime, often without a trial or any judicial process. It is an act of the legislative branch of government that imposes punishment, such as imprisonment or loss of property rights, on the designated person or group.

Article 3: Judicial Branch
- Section 1: Establishes the Supreme Court as the highest court in the land.

- Section 2: Defines the jurisdiction of the federal courts, including cases involving the Constitution, federal laws, and disputes between states.

- Section 3: Defines the crime of treason and the requirements for conviction.

Article 4: States' Relations
- Section 1: Addresses the Full Faith and Credit Clause[6], requiring states to honor the public acts, records, and judicial proceedings of other states.

- Section 2: Outlines the privileges and immunities[7] of citizens, extradition, and the return of escaped slaves.

- Section 3: Provides for the admission of new states and the control of federal territories.

- Section 4: Guarantees a republican form of government for the states[8] and protection against invasion and domestic violence.

Article 5: Amendment Process
- Outlines the process for proposing and ratifying amendments to the Constitution.

The process of amending the Constitution of the United States is outlined in Article V of the Constitution. **There are two primary methods by which amendments can be proposed and ratified:**

---

[6] The Full Faith and Credit Clause ensures that legal judgments, contracts, marriage licenses, property deeds, and other official documents and decisions made in one state are recognized and enforced in all other states. For example, if a person obtains a driver's license in one state, other states must recognize and honor that license, allowing the individual to legally drive across state lines.

[7] The Privileges and Immunities Clause prohibits states from discriminating against citizens of other states by denying them certain fundamental rights and privileges. It ensures that citizens from one state who are traveling, working, or residing in another state are entitled to the same legal protections, rights, and privileges as the residents of that state. The clause primarily applies to fundamental rights that are necessary for the functioning of a free and mobile society, such as the right to travel, the right to access the courts, the right to engage in employment, and the right to own property. It ensures that citizens are not treated unfairly or subjected to unreasonable burdens solely based on their state of residence.

[8] The term "republican form of government" refers to a representative form of government in which the power resides with the people who elect representatives to make decisions on their behalf. In a republican form of government, elected officials act as representatives of the citizens, and the government is constrained by a written constitution and the rule of law.

1. Proposal:
   - Amendment proposal by Congress: An amendment can be proposed by a two-thirds (supermajority) vote in both the Senate and the House of Representatives.
   - Amendment proposal by a constitutional convention: Upon application by two-thirds of the state legislatures (currently 34 out of 50 states), Congress must call a constitutional convention. However, this method has never been used to propose amendments.

2. Ratification[9]:
   - Amendment ratification by state legislatures: Once an amendment is proposed, it must be ratified by three-fourths (currently 38 out of 50) of the state legislatures. The state legislatures can either approve the amendment through a simple majority vote or by specifically called state conventions.
   - Amendment ratification by state conventions: Congress may choose to require the amendment to be ratified by state conventions rather than state legislatures. This method has only been used once for the ratification of the 21st Amendment, which repealed Prohibition.

To become part of the Constitution, an amendment must be ratified by the required number of states using one of the methods mentioned above. Once ratified, the amendment becomes an integral part of the Constitution and carries the same legal weight as any other provision.

The amendment process is intentionally designed to be a deliberate and cautious process, making it challenging to amend the Constitution. This ensures that any proposed changes have widespread support and are not subject to the whims of temporary political trends.

It's important to note that while the Constitution has been amended 27 times since its adoption, hundreds of proposed amendments have been introduced in Congress throughout the nation's history, but only a small fraction have successfully completed the amendment process.

Article 6: Supremacy Clause
- Establishes the Constitution and federal laws as the supreme law of the land.
- Requires state officials to take an oath of allegiance to the Constitution.

Article 7: Ratification
- Specifies the process for the ratification of the Constitution by the states.

---

[9] 26 of the 27 amendments were proposed by Congress and ratified by state legislatures. The 21st Amendment, which repealed Prohibition, was ratified by state conventions rather than state legislatures. This was the only amendment to use the method of amendment ratification by state conventions.

Here are the key steps and requirements of the ratification process:

Proposal of the Constitution:
The Constitution was proposed and drafted by the Constitutional Convention, which took place in Philadelphia in 1787. After months of deliberation and negotiation, the final version of the Constitution was produced and signed by the delegates.

Submission to the States:
Once the Constitution was finalized, it was submitted to the states for their consideration and approval. The Constitution was not directly sent to the existing state legislatures but instead to special state ratifying conventions.

Ratification by State Conventions:
The Constitution required that at least nine out of the thirteen states had to ratify it before it could come into effect. Each state held a special ratifying convention where elected delegates debated and voted on whether to accept or reject the Constitution.

Approval by State Conventions:
In each state convention, the delegates discussed the merits of the Constitution and its provisions. The Constitution had to be approved by a simple majority of the convention delegates in each state for ratification.

Rhode Island's Ratification:
Initially, only twelve states ratified the Constitution. However, for it to be fully effective and to include all thirteen states, the ratification by Rhode Island was necessary. Rhode Island initially resisted ratification but eventually ratified the Constitution in May 1790, more than two years after the initial ratifications.

Implementation:
After the required number of states ratified the Constitution, it came into effect. The new government established by the Constitution, including the three branches of the federal government (legislative, executive, and judicial), began operating under the Constitution's provisions.

Amendments to the Constitution

The amendments to the United States Constitution are an essential and equal part of the Constitution itself. They hold the same legal status and authority as the original text and play a vital role in shaping the nation's governance, protecting individual rights, and ensuring the Constitution's relevance and adaptability over time.

Amendment 1:

Text: "Congress shall make no law respecting an establishment of religion, or prohibiting the free exercise thereof; or abridging the freedom of speech, or of the press, or the right of the people peaceably to assemble, and to petition the Government for a redress of grievances."

Summary: Protects freedom of religion, speech, press, assembly, and the right to petition the government.

Amendment 2:

Text: "A well-regulated Militia, being necessary to the security of a free State, the right of the people to keep and bear Arms, shall not be infringed."

Summary: Guarantees the right of individuals to own and carry firearms.

Amendment 3:

Text: "No Soldier shall, in time of peace, be quartered in any house, without the consent of the Owner, nor in time of war but in a manner to be prescribed by law."

Summary: Prohibits the government from forcing homeowners to house soldiers during peacetime without their consent.

Amendment 4:

Text: "The right of the people to be secure in their persons, houses, papers, and effects, against unreasonable searches and seizures, shall not be violated, and no Warrants shall issue, but upon probable cause, supported by Oath or affirmation, and particularly describing the place to be searched, and the persons or things to be seized."

Summary: Protects against unreasonable searches and seizures and requires warrants based on probable cause.

Amendment 5:

Text: "No person shall be held to answer for a capital, or otherwise infamous crime, unless on a presentment or indictment of a Grand Jury, except in cases arising in the land or naval forces, or in the Militia, when in actual service in time of War or public danger; nor shall any person be subject for the same offence to be twice put in jeopardy of life or limb; nor shall be compelled in any criminal case to be a witness against himself, nor be deprived of life, liberty, or property, without due process of law; nor shall private property be taken for public use without just compensation."

Summary: Provides various protections for individuals accused of crimes, including the right to due process, protection against double jeopardy, and the right to remain silent.

Amendment 6:
Text: "In all criminal prosecutions, the accused shall enjoy the right to a speedy and public trial, by an impartial jury of the State and district wherein the crime shall have been committed, which district shall have been previously ascertained by law, and to be informed of the nature and cause of the accusation; to be confronted with the witnesses against him; to have compulsory process for obtaining witnesses in his favor, and to have the Assistance of Counsel for his defence."

Summary: Guarantees the right to a speedy and public trial, the right to an attorney, and the right to confront witnesses in criminal prosecutions.

Amendment 7:
Text: "In suits at common law, where the value in controversy shall exceed twenty dollars, the right of trial by jury shall be preserved, and no fact tried by a jury shall be otherwise re-examined in any court of the United States than according to the rules of the common law."

Summary: Ensures the right to a trial by jury in civil cases involving disputes over property or money exceeding a certain value.

Amendment 8:
Text: "Excessive bail shall not be required, nor excessive fines imposed, nor cruel and unusual punishments inflicted."

Summary: Prohibits excessive bail, fines, and cruel and unusual punishment.

Amendment 9:
Text: "The enumeration in the Constitution of certain rights shall not be construed to deny or disparage others retained by the people."

Summary: Protects rights not explicitly mentioned in the Constitution and ensures that these rights are not denied or diminished.

Amendment 10:
Text: "The powers not delegated to the United States by the Constitution, nor prohibited by it to the States, are reserved to the States respectively, or to the people."

Summary: Recognizes that powers not granted to the federal government nor prohibited to the states are reserved for the states or the people.

Amendment 11:
Text: "The Judicial power of the United States shall not be construed to extend to any suit in law or equity, commenced or prosecuted against one of the United States by Citizens of another State, or by Citizens or Subjects of any Foreign State."

Summary: Limits the ability of individuals to sue states in federal court.

Amendment 12:
Text: "The Electors shall meet in their respective states and vote by ballot for President and Vice-President, one of whom, at least, shall not be an inhabitant of the same state with themselves. They shall name in their ballots the person voted for as President, and in distinct ballots the person voted for as Vice-President, and they shall make distinct lists of all persons voted for as President, and all persons voted for as Vice-President, and of the number of votes for each, which lists they shall sign and certify, and transmit sealed to the seat of the government of the United States, directed to the President of the Senate."

Summary: Modifies the procedure for electing the President and Vice President by establishing separate ballots for each office.

Amendment 13:
Text: "Neither slavery nor involuntary servitude, except as a punishment for crime whereof the party shall have been duly convicted, shall exist within the United States, or any place subject to their jurisdiction."

Summary: Abolishes slavery and involuntary servitude, except as punishment for a crime.

Amendment 14:
Text: "All persons born or naturalized in the United States, and subject to the jurisdiction thereof, are citizens of the United States and of the State wherein they reside. No State shall make or enforce any law which shall abridge the privileges or

immunities of citizens of the United States; nor shall any State deprive any person of life, liberty, or property, without due process of law; nor deny to any person within its jurisdiction the equal protection of the laws."

Summary: Grants equal protection under the law to all citizens, defines citizenship, and ensures due process and equal treatment in the states.

Amendment 15:
Text: "The right of citizens of the United States to vote shall not be denied or abridged by the United States or by any State on account of race, color, or previous condition of servitude."

Summary: Prohibits the denial of voting rights based on race, color, or previous condition of servitude.

Amendment 16:
Text: "The Congress shall have power to lay and collect taxes on incomes, from whatever source derived, without apportionment among the several States, and without regard to any census or enumeration."

Summary: Authorizes Congress to levy an income tax.

Amendment 17:
Text: "The Senate of the United States shall be composed of two Senators from each State, elected by the people thereof, for six years; and each Senator shall have one vote. The electors in each State shall have the qualifications requisite for electors of the most numerous branch of the State legislatures."

Summary: Establishes the direct election of Senators by the people of each state.

Amendment 18:
Text: "After one year from the ratification of this article, the manufacture, sale, or transportation of intoxicating liquors within, the importation thereof into, or the exportation thereof from the United States and all territory subject to the jurisdiction thereof for beverage purposes is hereby prohibited."

Summary: Prohibited the manufacturing, sale, and transportation of alcoholic beverages (later repealed by the 21st Amendment).

Amendment 19:
Text: "The right of citizens of the United States to vote shall not be denied or abridged by the United States or by any State on account of sex."

Summary: Guarantees women the right to vote.

Amendment 20:
Text: "The terms of the President and Vice President shall end at noon on the 20th day of January, and the terms of Senators and Representatives at noon on the 3d day of January, of the years in which such terms would have ended if this article had not been ratified; and the terms of their successors shall then begin."

Summary: Changes the dates for the start of presidential and congressional terms.

Amendment 21:
Text: "The eighteenth article of amendment to the Constitution of the United States is hereby repealed."

Summary: Repeals the 18th Amendment, ending Prohibition.

Amendment 22:
Text: "No person shall be elected to the office of the President more than twice, and no person who has held the office of President, or acted as President, for more than two years of a term to which some other person was elected President shall be elected to the office of the President more than once."

Summary: Limits the President to two terms in office.

Amendment 23:
Text: "The District constituting the seat of Government of the United States shall appoint in such manner as the Congress may direct: A number of electors of President and Vice President equal to the whole number of Senators and Representatives in Congress to which the District would be entitled if it were a State, but in no event more than the least populous State; they shall be in addition to those appointed by the States, but they shall be considered, for the purposes of the election of President and Vice President, to be electors appointed by a State; and they shall meet in the District and perform such duties as provided by the twelfth article of amendment."

Summary: Grants residents of Washington, D.C., the right to vote in presidential elections.

Amendment 24:
Text: "The right of citizens of the United States to vote in any primary or other election for President or Vice President, for electors for President or Vice President, or for Senator or Representative in Congress, shall not be denied or

abridged by the United States or any State by reason of failure to pay any poll tax or other tax."

Summary: Prohibits the imposition of poll taxes as a condition for voting.

Amendment 25:
Text: "In case of the removal of the President from office or of his death or resignation, the Vice President shall become President."

Summary: Establishes procedures for the succession of the President and procedures for declaring the President unfit to serve.

Amendment 26:
Text: "The right of citizens of the United States, who are 18 years of age or older, to vote, shall not be denied or abridged by the United States or by any State on account of age."

Summary: Lowers the voting age from 21 to 18.

Amendment 27:
Text: "No law, varying the compensation for the services of the Senators and Representatives, shall take effect, until an election of Representatives shall have intervened."

Summary: Places restrictions on congressional pay increases, prohibiting any law changing congressional salaries from taking effect until the start of the next term.

Federalist Paper 10

To the People of the State of New York:

AMONG the numerous advantages promised by a well constructed Union, none deserves to be more accurately developed than its tendency to break and control the violence of faction. The friend of popular governments never finds himself so much alarmed for their character and fate, as when he contemplates their propensity to this dangerous vice. He will not fail, therefore, to set a due value on any plan which, without violating the principles to which he is attached, provides a proper cure for it. The instability, injustice, and confusion introduced into the public councils, have, in truth, been the mortal diseases under which popular governments have everywhere perished; as they continue to be the favorite and fruitful topics from which the adversaries to liberty derive their most specious declamations. The valuable improvements made by the American constitutions on the popular models, both ancient and modern, cannot certainly be too much admired; but it would be an unwarrantable partiality, to contend that they have as effectually obviated the danger on this side, as was wished and expected. Complaints are everywhere heard from our most considerate and virtuous citizens, equally the friends of public and private faith, and of public and personal liberty, that our governments are too unstable, that the public good is disregarded in the conflicts of rival parties, and that measures are too often decided, not according to the rules of justice and the rights of the minor party, but by the superior force of an interested and overbearing majority. However anxiously we may wish that these complaints had no foundation, the evidence, of known facts will not permit us to deny that they are in some degree true. It will be found, indeed, on a candid review of our situation, that some of the distresses under which we labor have been erroneously charged on the operation of our governments; but it will be found, at the same time, that other causes will not alone account for many of our heaviest misfortunes; and, particularly, for that prevailing and increasing distrust of public engagements, and alarm for private rights, which are echoed from one end of the continent to the other. These must be chiefly, if not wholly, effects of the unsteadiness and injustice with which a factious spirit has tainted our public administrations.

By a faction, I understand a number of citizens, whether amounting to a majority or a minority of the whole, who are united and actuated by some common impulse of passion, or of interest, adversed (opposed) to the rights of other citizens, or to the permanent and aggregate interests of the community.

There are two methods of curing the mischiefs of faction: the one, by removing its causes; the other, by controlling its effects.

There are again two methods of removing the causes of faction: the one, by destroying the liberty which is essential to its existence; the other, by giving to every citizen the same opinions, the same passions, and the same interests.

It could never be more truly said than of the first remedy, that it was worse than the disease. Liberty is to faction what air is to fire, an aliment without which it instantly expires. But it could not be less folly to abolish liberty, which is essential to political life, because it nourishes faction, than it would be to wish the annihilation of air, which is essential to animal life, because it imparts to fire its destructive agency.

The second expedient is as impracticable as the first would be unwise. As long as the reason of man continues to be fallible, and he is at liberty to exercise it, different opinions will be formed. As long as the connection subsists between his reason and his self-love, his opinions and his passions will have a reciprocal influence on each other; and the former will be objects to which the latter will attach themselves. The diversity in the faculties of men, from which the rights of property originate, is not less an insuperable obstacle to a uniformity of interests. The protection of these faculties is the first objective of the government. From the protection of different and unequal faculties of acquiring property, the possession of different degrees and kinds of property immediately results; and from the influence of these on the sentiments and views of the respective proprietors, ensues a division of the society into different interests and parties.

The latent causes of faction are thus sown in the nature of man; and we see them everywhere brought into different degrees of activity, according to the different circumstances of civil society. A zeal for different opinions concerning religion, concerning government, and many other points, as well of speculation as of practice; an attachment to different leaders ambitiously contending for pre-eminence and power; or to persons of other descriptions whose fortunes have been interesting to the human passions, have, in turn, divided mankind into parties, inflamed them with mutual animosity, and rendered them much more disposed to vex and oppress each other than to co-operate for their common good. So strong is this propensity of mankind to fall into mutual animosities, that where no substantial occasion presents itself, the most frivolous and fanciful distinctions have been sufficient to kindle their unfriendly passions and excite their most violent conflicts. But the most common and durable source of factions has been the various and unequal distribution of property. Those who hold and those who are without property have ever formed distinct interests in society. Those who are creditors, and those who are debtors, fall under a like discrimination. A landed interest, a manufacturing interest, a mercantile interest, a moneyed interest, with many lesser interests, grow up of necessity in civilized nations, and divide them into different classes, actuated by different sentiments and views. The regulation of these various and interfering interests forms the principal task of modern legislation, and involves the spirit of party and faction in the necessary and ordinary operations of the government.

No man is allowed to be a judge in his own cause, because his interest would certainly bias his judgment, and, not improbably, corrupt his integrity. With equal, nay with greater reason, a body of men are unfit to be both judges and parties at the same time; yet what are many of the most important acts of legislation, but so many judicial determinations, not indeed concerning the rights of single persons, but concerning the rights of large bodies of citizens? And what are the different classes of legislators but advocates and parties to the causes which they determine? Is a law proposed concerning private debts? It is a question to which the creditors are parties on one side and the debtors on the other. Justice ought to hold the balance between them. Yet the parties are, and must be, themselves the judges; and the most numerous party, or, in other words, the most powerful faction must be expected to prevail. Shall domestic manufactures be encouraged, and in what degree, by restrictions on foreign manufactures? are questions which would be differently decided by the landed and the manufacturing classes, and probably by neither with a sole regard to justice and the public good. The apportionment of taxes on the various descriptions of property is an act which seems to require the most exact impartiality; yet there is, perhaps, no legislative act in which greater opportunity and temptation are given to a predominant party to trample on the rules of justice. Every shilling with which they overburden the inferior number, is a shilling saved to their own pockets.

It is in vain to say that enlightened statesmen will be able to adjust these clashing interests, and render them all subservient to the public good. Enlightened statesmen will not always be at the helm. Nor, in many cases, can such an adjustment be made at all without taking into view indirect and remote considerations, which will rarely prevail over the immediate interest which one party may find in disregarding the rights of another or the good of the whole.

The inference to which we are brought is, that the CAUSES of faction cannot be removed, and that relief is only to be sought in the means of controlling its EFFECTS.

If a faction consists of less than a majority, relief is supplied by the republican principle, which enables the majority to defeat its sinister views by regular vote. It may clog the administration, it may convulse the society; but it will be unable to execute and mask its violence under the forms of the Constitution. When a majority is included in a faction, the form of popular government, on the other hand, enables it to sacrifice to its ruling passion or interest both the public good and the rights of other citizens. To secure the public good and private rights against the danger of such a faction, and at the same time to preserve the spirit and the form of popular government, is then the great object to which our inquiries are directed. Let me add that it is the great desideratum by which this form of government can be rescued from the opprobrium under which it has so long labored, and be recommended to the esteem and adoption of mankind.

By what means is this object attainable? Evidently by one of two only. Either the existence of the same passion or interest in a majority at the same time must be prevented, or the majority, having such coexistent passion or interest, must be rendered, by their number and local situation, unable to concert and carry into effect schemes of oppression. If the impulse and the opportunity be suffered to coincide, we well know that neither moral nor religious motives can be relied on as an adequate control. They are not found to be such on the injustice and violence of individuals, and lose their efficacy in proportion to the number combined together, that is, in proportion as their efficacy becomes needful.

From this view of the subject it may be concluded that a pure democracy, by which I mean a society consisting of a small number of citizens, who assemble and administer the government in person, can admit of no cure for the mischiefs of faction. A common passion or interest will, in almost every case, be felt by a majority of the whole; a communication and concert result from the form of government itself; and there is nothing to check the inducements to sacrifice the weaker party or an obnoxious individual. Hence it is that such democracies have ever been spectacles of turbulence and contention; have ever been found incompatible with personal security or the rights of property; and have in general been as short in their lives as they have been violent in their deaths. Theoretic politicians, who have patronized this species of government, have erroneously supposed that by reducing mankind to a perfect equality in their political rights, they would, at the same time, be perfectly equalized and assimilated in their possessions, their opinions, and their passions.

A republic, by which I mean a government in which the scheme of representation takes place, opens a different prospect, and promises the cure for which we are seeking. Let us examine the points in which it varies from pure democracy, and we shall comprehend both the nature of the cure and the efficacy which it must derive from the Union.

The two great points of difference between a democracy and a republic are: first, the delegation of the government, in the latter, to a small number of citizens elected by the rest; secondly, the greater number of citizens, and greater sphere of country, over which the latter may be extended.

The effect of the first difference is, on the one hand, to refine and enlarge the public views, by passing them through the medium of a chosen body of citizens, whose wisdom may best discern the true interest of their country, and whose patriotism and love of justice will be least likely to sacrifice it to temporary or partial considerations. Under such a regulation, it may well happen that the public voice, pronounced by the representatives of the people, will be more consonant to the public good than if pronounced by the people themselves, convened for the purpose. On the other hand, the effect may be inverted. Men of factious tempers, of local prejudices, or of sinister designs, may, by intrigue, by corruption, or by other means, first obtain the suffrages, and then betray the interests, of the people. The question resulting is, whether small or extensive republics are more favorable to the election of proper guardians of the public weal; and it is clearly decided in favor of the latter by two obvious considerations:

In the first place, it is to be remarked that, however small the republic may be, the representatives must be raised to a certain number, in order to guard against the cabals of a few; and that, however large it may be, they must be limited to a certain number, in order to guard against the confusion of a multitude. Hence, the number of representatives in the two cases not being in proportion to that of the two constituents, and being proportionally greater in the small republic, it follows that, if the proportion of fit characters be not less in the large than in the small republic, the former will present a greater option, and consequently a greater probability of a fit choice.

In the next place, as each representative will be chosen by a greater number of citizens in the large than in the small republic, it will be more difficult for unworthy candidates to practice with success the vicious arts by which elections are too often carried; and the suffrages of the people being more free, will be more likely to centre in men who possess the most attractive merit and the most diffusive and established characters.

It must be confessed that in this, as in most other cases, there is a mean, on both sides of which inconveniences will be found to lie. By enlarging too much the number of electors, you render the representatives too little acquainted with all their local circumstances and lesser interests; as by reducing it too much, you render him unduly attached to these, and too little fit to comprehend and pursue great and national objects. The federal Constitution forms a happy combination in this respect; the great and aggregate interests being referred to the national, the local and particular to the State legislatures.

The other point of difference is, the greater number of citizens and extent of territory which may be brought within the compass of republican than of democratic government; and it is this circumstance principally which renders factious combinations less to be dreaded in the former than in the latter. The smaller the society, the fewer probably will be the distinct parties and interests composing it; the fewer the distinct parties and interests, the more frequently will a majority be found of the same party; and the smaller the number of individuals composing a majority, and the smaller the compass within which they are placed, the more easily will they concert and execute their plans of oppression. Extend the sphere, and you take in a greater variety of parties and interests; you make it less probable that a majority of the whole will have a common motive to invade the rights of other citizens; or if such a common motive exists, it will be more difficult for all who feel it to discover their own strength, and to act in unison with each other. Besides other impediments, it may be remarked that, where there is a consciousness of unjust or dishonorable purposes, communication is always checked by distrust in proportion to the number whose concurrence is necessary.

Hence, it clearly appears, that the same advantage which a republic has over a democracy, in controlling the effects of faction, is enjoyed by a large over a small republic,--is enjoyed by the Union over the States composing it. Does the advantage consist in the substitution of representatives whose enlightened views and virtuous sentiments render them superior to local prejudices and schemes of injustice? It will not be denied that the representation of the Union will be most likely to possess these requisite endowments. Does it consist in the greater security afforded by a greater variety of parties, against the event of any one party being able to outnumber and oppress the rest? In an equal degree does the increased variety of parties comprised within the Union, increase this security. Does it, in fine, consist in the greater obstacles opposed to the concert and accomplishment of the secret wishes of an unjust and interested majority? Here, again, the extent of the Union gives it the most palpable advantage.

The influence of factious leaders may kindle a flame within their particular States, but will be unable to spread a general conflagration through the other States. A religious sect may degenerate into a political faction in a part of the Confederacy; but the variety of sects dispersed over the entire face of it must secure the national councils against any danger from that source. A rage for paper money, for an abolition of debts, for an equal division of property, or for any other improper or wicked project, will be less apt to pervade the whole body of the Union than a particular member of it; in the same proportion as such a malady is more likely to taint a particular county or district, than an entire State.

In the extent and proper structure of the Union, therefore, we behold a republican remedy for the diseases most incident to republican government. And according to the degree of pleasure and pride we feel in being republicans, ought to be our zeal in cherishing the spirit and supporting the character of Federalists.

PUBLIUS.

Outline of Federalist Paper 10

I. Introduction

    A. Context and purpose of the Federalist Papers

    B. Overview of the argument in Federalist Paper No. 10

II. Problem of Factions

    A. Definition of factions as groups with conflicting interests

    B. Concerns about the detrimental effects of factions on government and society

    C. Recognition that factions are inevitable in a free society

III. Causes and Control of Factions

    A. Explanation of the various causes of factions, including differing opinions, wealth, and personal interests

    B. Recognition that these causes cannot be eliminated or controlled by government

    C. Discussion of the dangers of majority factions and their potential to oppress minority rights

    D. Emphasis on the importance of controlling the effects of factions rather than eliminating them entirely

IV. Benefits of a Large Republic

    A. Advocacy for a large republic over a small one

B. Explanation of how a large republic can better control the effects of factions

C. Reflection on the diversity of interests and opinions in a large republic, making it more difficult for a single faction to dominate

D. Argument that a larger pool of representatives will result in a more balanced and fair representation of the people

V. Safeguards against Factions

A. Description of the constitutional structure as a safeguard against factions

B. Explanation of the separation of powers and checks and balances, preventing any one faction from gaining too much power

C. Advocacy for a representative democracy rather than a direct democracy to further mitigate the influence of factions

VI. Conclusion

A. Restatement of the importance of addressing the effects rather than the causes of factions

B. Reiteration of the benefits of a large republic in controlling factions

C. Assurance that the Constitution, with its checks and balances, provides a framework to protect the rights of all citizens while preventing factional tyranny

Federalist Paper 51

To the People of the State of New York:

TO WHAT expedient, then, shall we finally resort, for maintaining in practice the necessary partition of power among the several departments, as laid down in the Constitution? The only answer that can be given is, that as all these exterior provisions are found to be inadequate, the defect must be supplied, by so contriving the interior structure of the government as that its several constituent parts may, by their mutual relations, be the means of keeping each other in their proper places. Without presuming to undertake a full development of this important idea, I will hazard a few general observations, which may perhaps place it in a clearer light, and enable us to form a more correct judgment of the principles and structure of the government planned by the convention.

In order to lay a due foundation for that separate and distinct exercise of the different powers of government, which to a certain extent is admitted on all hands to be essential to the preservation of liberty, it is evident that each department should have a will of its own; and consequently should be so constituted that the members of each should have as little agency as possible in the appointment of the members of the others. Were this principle rigorously adhered to, it would require that all the appointments for the supreme executive, legislative, and judiciary magistracies should be drawn from the same fountain of authority, the people, through channels having no communication whatever with one another. Perhaps such a plan of constructing the several departments would be less difficult in practice than it may in contemplation appear. Some difficulties, however, and some additional expense would attend the execution of it. Some deviations, therefore, from the principle must be admitted. In the constitution of the judiciary department in particular, it might be inexpedient to insist rigorously on the principle: first, because peculiar qualifications being essential in the members, the primary consideration ought to be to select that mode of choice which best secures these qualifications; secondly, because the permanent tenure by which the appointments are held in that department, must soon destroy all sense of dependence on the authority conferring them.

It is equally evident, that the members of each department should be as little dependent as possible on those of the others, for the emoluments annexed to their offices. Were the executive magistrate, or the judges, not independent of the legislature in this particular, their independence in every other would be merely nominal. But the great security against a gradual concentration of the several powers in the same department, consists in giving to those who administer each department the necessary constitutional means and personal motives to resist encroachments of the others. The provision for defense must in this, as in all other cases, be made commensurate to the danger of attack. Ambition must be made to counteract ambition. The interest of the man must be connected with the constitutional rights of the place. It may be a reflection on human nature, that such devices should be necessary to control the abuses of government. But what is government itself, but the greatest of all reflections on human nature? If men were angels, no government would be necessary. If angels were to govern men, neither external nor internal controls on government would be necessary. In framing a government which is to be administered by men over men, the great difficulty lies in this: you must first enable the government to control the governed; and in the next place oblige it to control itself.

A dependence on the people is, no doubt, the primary control on the government; but experience has taught mankind the necessity of auxiliary precautions. This policy of supplying, by opposite and rival interests, the defect of better motives, might be traced through the whole system of human affairs, private as well as public. We see it particularly displayed in all the subordinate distributions of power, where the constant aim is to divide and arrange the several offices in such a manner as that each may be a check on the other that the private interest of every individual may be a sentinel over the public rights. These inventions of prudence cannot be less requisite in the distribution of the supreme powers of the State. But it is not possible to give to each department an equal power of self-defense. In republican government, the legislative authority necessarily predominates. The remedy for this inconveniency is to divide the legislature into different branches; and to render them, by different modes of election and different principles of action, as little connected with each other as the nature of their common functions and their common dependence on the society will admit. It may even be necessary to guard against dangerous encroachments by still further precautions. As the weight of the legislative authority requires that it should be thus divided, the weakness of the executive may require, on the other hand, that it should be fortified.

An absolute negative on the legislature appears, at first view, to be the natural defense with which the executive magistrate should be armed. But perhaps it would be neither altogether safe nor alone sufficient. On ordinary occasions it might not be exerted with the requisite firmness, and on extraordinary occasions it might be perfidiously abused. May not this defect of an absolute negative be supplied by some qualified connection between this weaker department and the weaker branch of the stronger department, by which the latter may be led to support the constitutional rights of the former, without being too much detached from the rights of its own department? If the principles on which these observations are founded be just, as I persuade myself they are, and they be applied as a criterion to the several State constitutions, and to the federal Constitution it will be found that if the latter does not perfectly correspond with them, the former are infinitely less able to bear such a test.

There are, moreover, two considerations particularly applicable to the federal system of America, which place that system in a very interesting point of view. First. In a single republic, all the power surrendered by the people is submitted to the administration of a single government; and the usurpations are guarded against by a division of the government into distinct and separate departments. In the compound republic of America, the power surrendered by the people is first divided between two distinct governments, and then the portion allotted to each subdivided among distinct and separate departments. Hence a double security arises to the rights of the people. The different governments will control each other, at the same time that each will be controlled by itself. Second. It is of great importance in a republic not only to guard the society against the oppression of its rulers, but to guard one part of the society against the injustice of the other part. Different interests necessarily exist in different classes of citizens. If a majority be united by a common interest, the rights of the minority will be insecure.

There are but two methods of providing against this evil: the one by creating a will in the community independent of the majority that is, of the society itself; the other, by comprehending in the society so many separate descriptions of citizens as will render an unjust combination of a majority of the whole very improbable, if not impracticable. The first method prevails in all governments possessing an hereditary or self-appointed authority. This, at best, is but a precarious security; because a power independent of the society may as well espouse the unjust views of the major, as the rightful interests of the minor party, and may possibly be turned against both parties. The second method will be exemplified in the federal republic of the United States. Whilst all authority in it will be derived from and dependent on the society, the society itself will be broken into so many parts, interests, and classes of citizens, that the rights of individuals, or of the minority, will be in little danger from interested combinations of the majority.

In a free government the security for civil rights must be the same as that for religious rights. It consists in the one case in the multiplicity of interests, and in the other in the multiplicity of sects. The degree of security in both cases will depend on the number of interests and sects; and this may be presumed to depend on the extent of country and number of people comprehended under the same government. This view of the subject must particularly recommend a proper federal system to all the sincere and considerate friends of republican government, since it shows that in exact proportion as the territory of the Union may be formed into more circumscribed Confederacies, or States oppressive combinations of a majority will be facilitated: the best security, under the republican forms, for the rights of every class of citizens, will be diminished: and consequently the stability and independence of some member of the government, the only other security, must be proportionately increased. Justice is the end of government. It is the end of civil society. It ever has been and ever will be pursued until it be obtained, or until liberty be lost in the pursuit. In a society under the forms of which the stronger faction can readily unite and oppress the weaker, anarchy may as truly be said to reign as in a state of nature, where the weaker individual is not secured against the violence of the stronger; and as, in the latter state, even the stronger individuals are prompted, by the uncertainty of their condition, to submit to a government which may protect the weak as well as themselves; so, in the former state, will the more powerful factions or parties be gradnally induced, by a like motive, to wish for a government which will protect all parties, the weaker as well as the more powerful.

It can be little doubted that if the State of Rhode Island was separated from the Confederacy and left to itself, the insecurity of rights under the popular form of government within such narrow limits would be displayed by such reiterated oppressions of factious majorities that some power altogether independent of the people would soon be called for by the voice of the very factions whose misrule had proved the necessity of it. In the extended republic of the United States, and among the great variety of interests, parties, and sects which it embraces, a coalition of a majority of the whole society could seldom take place on any other principles than those of justice and the general good; whilst there being thus less danger to a minor from the will of a major party, there must be less pretext, also, to provide for the security of the former, by introducing into the government a will not dependent on the latter, or, in other words, a will independent of the society itself. It is no less certain than it is important, notwithstanding the contrary opinions which have been entertained, that the larger the society, provided it lie within a practical sphere, the more duly capable it will be of self-government. And happily for the REPUBLICAN CAUSE, the practicable sphere may be carried to a very great extent, by a judicious modification and mixture of the FEDERAL PRINCIPLE.

PUBLIUS.

Outline of Federalist Paper No. 51

I. Introduction
    A. The importance of the separation of powers and checks and balances

    B. The structure and purpose of the paper

II. Background on Human Nature and Government

    A. Human nature is inclined to pursue self-interest

    B. Government is necessary to control the effects of these inclinations

    C. Ambition must be made to counteract ambition

III. The Structure of the Government

    A. Government should be divided into separate departments
      1. Legislative, executive, and judicial branches

      2. Each branch with distinct powers and responsibilities

    B. Each branch should be independent and have a will of its own
      1. Prevents one branch from dominating the others

      2. Protects against tyranny

IV. The Legislative Branch

    A. Most powerful branch due to representation of the people

    B. Bicameral legislature to create further checks and balances

    C. Each chamber with different qualifications and modes of selection

    D. Encourages deliberation and acts as a safeguard against hasty decisions

V. The Executive Branch

    A. Necessity of a strong executive to ensure enforcement of laws

B. The method of selection for the executive

    1. Arguments for and against popular election

    2. Compromise: Electoral College

C. Powers and responsibilities of the executive

    1. Commander-in-Chief, veto power, appointment of officials

D. Impeachment as a check on executive misconduct

VI. The Judicial Branch

A. The role of an independent judiciary

B. Judges' tenure and mode of appointment to ensure impartiality

C. Judicial review to protect the Constitution and check legislative acts

VII. Checks and Balances

A. Each branch has constitutional means to resist encroachment by others

B. The people also serve as a check through representation and elections

C. Encourages negotiation, compromise, and moderation

VIII. Conclusion

A. The importance of the separation of powers and checks and balances

B. The need for a strong government that can control itself

Federalist Paper 70

To the People of the State of New York:

THERE is an idea, which is not without its advocates, that a vigorous Executive is inconsistent with the genius of republican government. The enlightened well-wishers to this species of government must at least hope that the supposition is destitute of foundation; since they can never admit its truth, without at the same time admitting the condemnation of their own principles. Energy in the Executive is a leading character in the definition of good government. It is essential to the protection of the community against foreign attacks; it is not less essential to the steady administration of the laws; to the protection of property against those irregular and high-handed combinations which sometimes interrupt the ordinary course of justice; to the security of liberty against the enterprises and assaults of ambition, of faction, and of anarchy. Every man the least conversant in Roman story, knows how often that republic was obliged to take refuge in the absolute power of a single man, under the formidable title of Dictator, as well against the intrigues of ambitious individuals who aspired to the tyranny, and the seditions of whole classes of the community whose conduct threatened the existence of all government, as against the invasions of external enemies who menaced the conquest and destruction of Rome.

There can be no need, however, to multiply arguments or examples on this head. A feeble Executive implies a feeble execution of the government. A feeble execution is but another phrase for a bad execution; and a government ill executed, whatever it may be in theory, must be, in practice, a bad government.

Taking it for granted, therefore, that all men of sense will agree in the necessity of an energetic Executive, it will only remain to inquire, what are the ingredients which constitute this energy? How far can they be combined with those other ingredients which constitute safety in the republican sense? And how far does this combination characterize the plan which has been reported by the convention?

The ingredients which constitute energy in the Executive are, first, unity; secondly, duration; thirdly, an adequate provision for its support; fourthly, competent powers.

The ingredients which constitute safety in the republican sense are, first, a due dependence on the people, secondly, a due responsibility.

Those politicians and statesmen who have been the most celebrated for the soundness of their principles and for the justice of their views, have declared in favor of a single Executive and a numerous legislature. They have with great propriety, considered energy as the most necessary qualification of the former, and have regarded this as most applicable to power in a single hand, while they have, with equal propriety, considered the latter as best adapted to deliberation and wisdom, and best calculated to conciliate the confidence of the people and to secure their privileges and interests.

That unity is conducive to energy will not be disputed. Decision, activity, secrecy, and despatch will generally characterize the proceedings of one man in a much more eminent degree than the proceedings of any greater number; and in proportion as the number is increased, these qualities will be diminished.

This unity may be destroyed in two ways: either by vesting the power in two or more magistrates of equal dignity and authority; or by vesting it ostensibly in one man, subject, in whole or in part, to the control and co-operation of others, in the capacity of counsellors to him. Of the first, the two Consuls of Rome may serve as an example; of the last, we shall find examples in the constitutions of several of the States. New York and New Jersey, if I recollect right, are the only States which have intrusted the executive authority wholly to single men. Both these methods of destroying the unity of the Executive have their partisans; but the votaries of an executive council are the most numerous. They are both liable, if not to equal, to similar objections, and may in most lights be examined in conjunction.

The experience of other nations will afford little instruction on this head. As far, however, as it teaches any thing, it teaches us not to be enamoured of plurality in the Executive. We have seen that the Achaeans, on an experiment of two Praetors, were induced to abolish one. The Roman history records many instances of mischiefs to the republic from the dissensions between the Consuls, and between the military Tribunes, who were at times substituted for the Consuls. But it gives us no specimens of any peculiar advantages derived to the state from the circumstance of the plurality of those magistrates. That the dissensions between them were not more frequent or more fatal, is a matter of astonishment, until we advert to the singular position in which the republic was almost continually placed, and to the prudent policy pointed out by the circumstances of the state, and pursued by the Consuls, of making a division of the government between them. The patricians engaged in a perpetual struggle with the plebeians for the preservation of their ancient authorities and dignities; the Consuls, who were generally chosen out of the former body, were commonly united by the personal interest they had in the defense of the privileges of their order. In addition to this motive of union, after the arms of the republic had considerably expanded the bounds of its empire, it became an established custom with the Consuls to divide the administration between themselves by lot — one of them remaining at Rome to govern the city and its environs, the other taking the command in the more distant provinces. This expedient must, no doubt, have had great influence in preventing those collisions and rivalships which might otherwise have embroiled the peace of the republic.

But quitting the dim light of historical research, attaching ourselves purely to the dictates of reason and good sense, we shall discover much greater cause to reject than to approve the idea of plurality in the Executive, under any modification whatever.

Wherever two or more persons are engaged in any common enterprise or pursuit, there is always danger of difference of opinion. If it be a public trust or office, in which they are clothed with equal dignity and authority, there is peculiar danger of personal emulation and even animosity. From either, and especially from all these causes, the most bitter dissensions are apt to spring. Whenever these happen, they lessen the respectability, weaken the authority, and distract the plans and operation of those whom they divide. If they should unfortunately assail the supreme executive magistracy of a country, consisting of a plurality of persons, they might impede or frustrate the most important measures of the government, in the most critical emergencies of the state. And what is still worse, they might split the community into the most violent and irreconcilable factions, adhering differently to the different individuals who composed the magistracy.

Men often oppose a thing, merely because they have had no agency in planning it, or because it may have been planned by those whom they dislike. But if they have been consulted, and have happened to disapprove, opposition then becomes, in their estimation, an indispensable duty of self-love. They seem to think themselves bound in honor, and by all the motives of personal infallibility, to defeat the success of what has been resolved upon contrary to their sentiments. Men of upright, benevolent tempers have too many opportunities of remarking, with horror, to what desperate lengths this disposition is sometimes carried, and how often the great interests of society are sacrificed to the vanity, to the conceit, and to the obstinacy of individuals, who have credit enough to make their passions and their caprices interesting to mankind. Perhaps the question now before the public may, in its consequences, afford melancholy proofs of the effects of this despicable frailty, or rather detestable vice, in the human character.

Upon the principles of a free government, inconveniences from the source just mentioned must necessarily be submitted to in the formation of the legislature; but it is unnecessary, and therefore unwise, to introduce them into the constitution of the Executive. It is here too that they may be most pernicious. In the legislature, promptitude of decision is oftener an evil than a benefit. The differences of opinion, and the jarrings of parties in that department of the government, though they may sometimes obstruct salutary plans, yet often promote deliberation and circumspection, and serve to check excesses in the majority. When a resolution too is once taken, the opposition must be at an end. That resolution is a law, and resistance to it punishable. But no favorable circumstances palliate or atone for the disadvantages of dissension in the executive department. Here, they are pure and unmixed. There is no point at which they cease to operate. They serve to embarrass and weaken the execution of the plan or measure to which they relate, from the first step to the final conclusion of it. They constantly counteract those qualities in the Executive which are the most necessary ingredients in its composition — vigor and expedition, and this without any counterbalancing good. In the conduct of war, in which the energy of the Executive is the bulwark of the national security, everything would be to be apprehended from its plurality.

It must be confessed that these observations apply with principal weight to the first case supposed — that is, to a plurality of magistrates of equal dignity and authority a scheme, the advocates for which are not likely to form a numerous sect; but they apply, though not with equal, yet with considerable weight to the project of a council, whose concurrence is made constitutionally necessary to the operations of the ostensible Executive. An artful cabal in that council would be able to distract and to enervate the whole system of administration. If no such cabal should exist, the mere diversity of views and opinions would alone be sufficient to tincture the exercise of the executive authority with a spirit of habitual feebleness and dilatoriness.

But one of the weightiest objections to a plurality in the Executive, and which lies as much against the last as the first plan, is, that it tends to conceal faults and destroy responsibility.

Responsibility is of two kinds — to censure and to punishment. The first is the more important of the two, especially in an elective office. Man, in public trust, will much oftener act in such a manner as to render him unworthy of being any longer trusted, than in such a manner as to make him obnoxious to legal punishment. But the multiplication of the Executive adds to the difficulty of detection in either case. It often becomes impossible, amidst mutual accusations, to determine on whom the blame or the punishment of a pernicious measure, or series of pernicious measures, ought really to fall. It is shifted from one to another with so much dexterity, and under such plausible appearances, that the public opinion is left in suspense about the real author. The circumstances which may have led to any national miscarriage or misfortune are sometimes so complicated that, where there are a number of actors who may have had different degrees and kinds of agency, though we may clearly see upon the whole that there has been mismanagement, yet it may be impracticable to pronounce to whose account the evil which may have been incurred is truly chargeable.

"I was overruled by my council. The council were so divided in their opinions that it was impossible to obtain any better resolution on the point." These and similar pretexts are constantly at hand, whether true or false. And who is there that will either take the trouble or incur the odium, of a strict scrunity into the secret springs of the transaction? Should there be found a citizen zealous enough to undertake the unpromising task, if there happen to be collusion between the parties concerned, how easy it is to clothe the circumstances with so much ambiguity, as to render it uncertain what was the precise conduct of any of those parties?

In the single instance in which the governor of this State is coupled with a council — that is, in the appointment to offices, we have seen the mischiefs of it in the view now under consideration. Scandalous appointments to important offices have been made. Some cases, indeed, have been so flagrant that ALL PARTIES have agreed in the impropriety of the thing. When inquiry has been made, the blame has been laid by the governor on the members of the council, who, on their part, have charged it upon his nomination; while the people remain altogether at a loss to determine, by whose influence their interests have been committed to hands so unqualified and so manifestly improper. In tenderness to individuals, I forbear to descend to particulars.

It is evident from these considerations, that the plurality of the Executive tends to deprive the people of the two greatest securities they can have for the faithful exercise of any delegated power, first, the restraints of public opinion, which lose their efficacy, as well on account of the division of the censure attendant on bad measures among a number, as on account of the uncertainty on whom it ought to fall; and, second, the opportunity of discovering with facility and clearness the misconduct of the persons they trust, in order either to their removal from office or to their actual punishment in cases which admit of it.

In England, the king is a perpetual magistrate; and it is a maxim which has obtained for the sake of the public peace, that he is unaccountable for his administration, and his person sacred. Nothing, therefore, can be wiser in that kingdom, than to annex to the king a constitutional council, who may be responsible to the nation for the advice they give. Without this, there would be no responsibility whatever in the executive department — an idea inadmissible in a free government. But even there the king is not bound by the resolutions of his council, though they are answerable for the advice they give. He is the absolute master of his own conduct in the exercise of his office, and may observe or disregard the counsel given to him at his sole discretion.

But in a republic, where every magistrate ought to be personally responsible for his behavior in office the reason which in the British Constitution dictates the propriety of a council, not only ceases to apply, but turns against the institution. In the monarchy of Great Britain, it furnishes a substitute for the prohibited responsibility of the chief magistrate, which serves in some degree as a hostage to the national justice for his good behavior. In the American republic, it would serve to destroy, or would greatly diminish, the intended and necessary responsibility of the Chief Magistrate himself.

The idea of a council to the Executive, which has so generally obtained in the State constitutions, has been derived from that maxim of republican jealousy which considers power as safer in the hands of a number of men than of a single man. If the maxim should be admitted to be applicable to the case, I should contend that the advantage on that side would not counterbalance the numerous disadvantages on the opposite side. But I do not think the rule at all applicable to the executive power. I clearly concur in opinion, in this particular, with a writer whom the celebrated Junius pronounces to be "deep, solid, and ingenious," that "the executive power is more easily confined when it is ONE"; that it is far more safe there should be a single object for the jealousy and watchfulness of the people; and, in a word, that all multiplication of the Executive is rather dangerous than friendly to liberty.

A little consideration will satisfy us, that the species of security sought for in the multiplication of the Executive, is unattainable. Numbers must be so great as to render combination difficult, or they are rather a source of danger than of security. The united credit and influence of several individuals must be more formidable to liberty, than the credit and influence of either of them separately. When power, therefore, is placed in the hands of so small a number of men, as to admit of their interests and views being easily combined in a common enterprise, by an artful leader, it becomes more liable to abuse, and more dangerous when abused, than if it be lodged in the hands of one man; who, from the very circumstance of his being alone, will be more narrowly watched and more readily suspected, and who cannot unite so great a mass of influence as when he is associated with others. The Decemvirs of Rome, whose name denotes their number, 3 were more to be dreaded in their usurpation than any ONE of them would have been. No person would think of proposing an Executive much more numerous than that body; from six to a dozen have been suggested for the number of the council. The extreme of these numbers, is not too great for an easy combination; and from such a combination America would have more to fear, than from the ambition of any single individual. A council to a magistrate, who is himself responsible for what he does, are generally nothing better than a clog upon his good intentions, are often the instruments and accomplices of his bad and are almost always a cloak to his faults.

I forbear to dwell upon the subject of expense; though it be evident that if the council should be numerous enough to answer the principal end aimed at by the institution, the salaries of the members, who must be drawn from their homes to reside at the seat of government, would form an item in the catalogue of public expenditures too serious to be incurred for an object of equivocal utility. I will only add that, prior to the appearance of the Constitution, I rarely met with an intelligent man from any of the States, who did not admit, as the result of experience, that the UNITY of the executive of this State was one of the best of the distinguishing features of our constitution.
PUBLIUS.

Outline of Federalist 70

I. Introduction

    A. Importance of an energetic executive

    B. Examination of the nature and benefits of a strong executive

    C. Contrast with other branches of government

II. The Unity of the Executive

    A. Advantage of having a single executive

    B. Avoiding conflicts and promoting efficient decision-making

    C. Comparisons to multiple executives in state governments

III. Energy in the Executive

    A. The need for prompt and decisive action

    B. Protection against foreign threats and the role of the executive

    C. Comparison to the executive power in the British monarchy

IV. Duration in Office

    A. The benefits of a fixed term for the executive

    B. Considerations on re-election and accountability

    C. Reflecting on the balance between stability and responsiveness

V. Conclusion

   A. Summary of the arguments for an energetic executive

   B. The importance of an independent and effective executive branch

   C. Assurance of liberty and protection of the nation

Throughout Federalist Paper No. 70, Hamilton argues that a strong and energetic executive is necessary for the proper functioning of the government. He emphasizes the unity, energy, and duration in office as crucial aspects of the executive branch. Hamilton also discusses the importance of prompt decision-making, protection against foreign threats, and the balance between stability and accountability. The paper ultimately highlights the role of an independent and effective executive in safeguarding liberty and ensuring the well-being of the nation.

Federalist 78

To the People of the State of New York:

WE PROCEED now to an examination of the judiciary department of the proposed government.

In unfolding the defects of the existing Confederation, the utility and necessity of a federal judicature have been clearly pointed out. It is the less necessary to recapitulate the considerations there urged, as the propriety of the institution in the abstract is not disputed; the only questions which have been raised being relative to the manner of constituting it, and to its extent. To these points, therefore, our observations shall be confined.

The manner of constituting it seems to embrace these several objects: 1st. The mode of appointing the judges. 2d. The tenure by which they are to hold their places. 3d. The partition of the judiciary authority between different courts, and their relations to each other.

First. As to the mode of appointing the judges; this is the same with that of appointing the officers of the Union in general, and has been so fully discussed in the two last numbers, that nothing can be said here which would not be useless repetition.

Second. As to the tenure by which the judges are to hold their places; this chiefly concerns their duration in office; the provisions for their support; the precautions for their responsibility.

According to the plan of the convention, all judges who may be appointed by the United States are to hold their offices DURING GOOD BEHAVIOR; which is conformable to the most approved of the State constitutions and among the rest, to that of this State. Its propriety having been drawn into question by the adversaries of that plan, is no light symptom of the rage for objection, which disorders their imaginations and judgments. The standard of good behavior for the continuance in office of the judicial magistracy, is certainly one of the most valuable of the modern improvements in the practice of government. In a monarchy it is an excellent barrier to the despotism of the prince; in a republic it is a no less excellent barrier to the encroachments and oppressions of the representative body. And it is the best expedient which can be devised in any government, to secure a steady, upright, and impartial administration of the laws.

Whoever attentively considers the different departments of power must perceive, that, in a government in which they are separated from each other, the judiciary, from the nature of its functions, will always be the least dangerous to the political rights of the Constitution; because it will be least in a capacity to annoy or injure them. The Executive not only dispenses the honors, but holds the sword of the community. The legislature not only commands the purse, but prescribes the rules by which the duties and rights of every citizen are to be regulated. The judiciary, on the contrary, has no influence over either the sword or the purse; no direction either of the strength or of the wealth of the society; and can take no active resolution whatever. It may truly be said to have neither FORCE nor WILL, but merely judgment; and must ultimately depend upon the aid of the executive arm even for the efficacy of its judgments.

This simple view of the matter suggests several important consequences. It proves incontestably, that the judiciary is beyond comparison the weakest of the three departments of power1; that it can never attack with success either of the other two; and that all possible care is requisite to enable it to defend itself against their attacks. It equally proves, that though individual oppression may now and then proceed from the courts of justice, the general liberty of the people can never be endangered from that quarter; I mean so long as the judiciary remains truly distinct from both the legislature and the Executive. For I agree, that "there is no liberty, if the power of judging be not separated from the legislative and executive powers."2 And it proves, in the last place, that as liberty can have nothing to fear from the judiciary alone, but would have every thing to fear from its union with either of the other departments; that as all the effects of such a union must ensue from a dependence of the former on the latter, notwithstanding a nominal and apparent separation; that as, from the natural feebleness of the judiciary, it is in continual jeopardy of being overpowered, awed, or influenced by its co-ordinate branches; and that as nothing can contribute so much to its firmness and independence as permanency in office, this quality may therefore be justly regarded as an indispensable ingredient in its constitution, and, in a great measure, as the citadel of the public justice and the public security.

The complete independence of the courts of justice is peculiarly essential in a limited Constitution. By a limited Constitution, I understand one which contains certain specified exceptions to the legislative authority; such, for instance, as that it shall pass no bills of attainder, no ex-post-facto laws, and the like. Limitations of this kind can be preserved in practice no other way than through the medium of courts of justice, whose duty it must be to declare all acts contrary to the manifest tenor of the Constitution void. Without this, all the reservations of particular rights or privileges would amount to nothing.

Some perplexity respecting the rights of the courts to pronounce legislative acts void, because contrary to the Constitution, has arisen from an imagination that the doctrine would imply a superiority of the judiciary to the legislative power. It is urged that the authority which can declare the acts of another void, must necessarily be superior to the one whose acts may be declared void. As this doctrine is of great importance in all the American constitutions, a brief discussion of the ground on which it rests cannot be unacceptable.

There is no position which depends on clearer principles, than that every act of a delegated authority, contrary to the tenor of the commission under which it is exercised, is void. No legislative act, therefore, contrary to the Constitution, can be valid. To deny this, would be to affirm, that the deputy is greater than his principal; that the servant is above his master; that the representatives of the people are superior to the people themselves; that men acting by virtue of powers, may do not only what their powers do not authorize, but what they forbid.

If it be said that the legislative body are themselves the constitutional judges of their own powers, and that the construction they put upon them is conclusive upon the other departments, it may be answered, that this cannot be the natural presumption, where it is not to be collected from any particular provisions in the Constitution. It is not otherwise to be supposed, that the Constitution could intend to enable the representatives of the people to substitute their WILL to that of their constituents. It is far more rational to suppose, that the courts were designed to be an intermediate body between the people and the legislature, in order, among other things, to keep the latter within the limits assigned to their authority. The interpretation of the laws is the proper and peculiar province of the courts. A constitution is, in fact, and must be regarded by the judges, as a fundamental law. It therefore belongs to them to ascertain its meaning, as well as the meaning of any particular act proceeding from the legislative body. If there should happen to be an irreconcilable variance between the two, that which has the superior obligation and validity ought, of course, to be preferred; or, in other words, the Constitution ought to be preferred to the statute, the intention of the people to the intention of their agents.

Nor does this conclusion by any means suppose a superiority of the judicial to the legislative power. It only supposes that the power of the people is superior to both; and that where the will of the legislature, declared in its statutes, stands in opposition to that of the people, declared in the Constitution, the judges ought to be governed by the latter rather than the former. They ought to regulate their decisions by the fundamental laws, rather than by those which are not fundamental.

This exercise of judicial discretion, in determining between two contradictory laws, is exemplified in a familiar instance. It not uncommonly happens, that there are two statutes existing at one time, clashing in whole or in part with each other, and neither of them containing any repealing clause or expression. In such a case, it is the province of the courts to liquidate and fix their meaning and operation. So far as they can, by any fair construction, be reconciled to each other, reason and law conspire to dictate that this should be done; where this is impracticable, it becomes a matter of necessity to give effect to one, in exclusion of the other. The rule which has obtained in the courts for determining their relative validity is, that the last in order of time shall be preferred to the first. But this is a mere rule of construction, not derived from any positive law, but from the nature and reason of the thing. It is a rule not enjoined upon the courts by legislative provision, but adopted by themselves, as consonant to truth and propriety, for the direction of their conduct as interpreters of the law. They thought it reasonable, that between the interfering acts of an EQUAL authority, that which was the last indication of its will should have the preference.

But in regard to the interfering acts of a superior and subordinate authority, of an original and derivative power, the nature and reason of the thing indicate the converse of that rule as proper to be followed. They teach us that the prior act of a superior ought to be preferred to the subsequent act of an inferior and subordinate authority; and that accordingly, whenever a particular statute contravenes the Constitution, it will be the duty of the judicial tribunals to adhere to the latter and disregard the former.

It can be of no weight to say that the courts, on the pretense of a repugnancy, may substitute their own pleasure to the constitutional intentions of the legislature. This might as well happen in the case of two contradictory statutes; or it might as well happen in every adjudication upon any single statute. The courts must declare the sense of the law; and if they should be disposed to exercise WILL instead of JUDGMENT, the consequence would equally be the substitution of their pleasure to that of the legislative body. The observation, if it prove any thing, would prove that there ought to be no judges distinct from that body.

If, then, the courts of justice are to be considered as the bulwarks of a limited Constitution against legislative encroachments, this consideration will afford a strong argument for the permanent tenure of judicial offices, since nothing will contribute so much as this to that independent spirit in the judges which must be essential to the faithful performance of so arduous a duty.

This independence of the judges is equally requisite to guard the Constitution and the rights of individuals from the effects of those ill humors, which the arts of designing men, or the influence of particular conjunctures, sometimes disseminate among the people themselves, and which, though they speedily give place to better information, and more deliberate reflection, have a tendency, in the meantime, to occasion dangerous innovations in the government, and serious oppressions of the minor party in the community. Though I trust the friends of the proposed Constitution will never concur with its enemies,3 in questioning that fundamental principle of republican government, which admits the right of the people to alter or abolish the established Constitution, whenever they find it inconsistent with their happiness, yet it is not to be inferred from this principle, that the representatives of the people, whenever a momentary inclination happens to lay hold of a majority of their constituents, incompatible with the provisions in the existing Constitution, would, on that account, be justifiable in a violation of those provisions; or that the courts would be under a greater obligation to connive at infractions in this shape, than when they had proceeded wholly from the cabals of the representative body. Until the people have, by some solemn and authoritative act, annulled or changed the established form, it is binding upon themselves collectively, as well as individually; and no presumption, or even knowledge, of their sentiments, can warrant their representatives in a departure from it, prior to such an act. But it is easy to see, that it would require an uncommon portion of fortitude in the judges to do their duty as faithful guardians of the Constitution, where legislative invasions of it had been instigated by the major voice of the community.

But it is not with a view to infractions of the Constitution only, that the independence of the judges may be an essential safeguard against the effects of occasional ill humors in the society. These sometimes extend no farther than to the injury of the private rights of particular classes of citizens, by unjust and partial laws. Here also the firmness of the judicial magistracy is of vast importance in mitigating the severity and confining the operation of such laws. It not only serves to moderate the immediate mischiefs of those which may have been passed, but it operates as a check upon the legislative body in passing them; who, perceiving that obstacles to the success of iniquitous intention are to be expected from the scruples of the courts, are in a manner compelled, by the very motives of the injustice they meditate, to qualify their attempts. This is a circumstance calculated to have more influence upon the character of our governments, than but few may be aware of. The benefits of the integrity and moderation of the judiciary have already been felt in more States than one; and though they may have displeased those whose sinister expectations they may have disappointed, they must have commanded the esteem and applause of all the virtuous and disinterested. Considerate men, of every description, ought to prize whatever will tend to beget or fortify that temper in the courts: as no man can be sure that he may not be to-morrow the victim of a spirit of injustice, by which he may be a gainer to-day. And every man must now feel, that the inevitable tendency of such a spirit is to sap the foundations of public and private confidence, and to introduce in its stead universal distrust and distress.

That inflexible and uniform adherence to the rights of the Constitution, and of individuals, which we perceive to be indispensable in the courts of justice, can certainly not be expected from judges who hold their offices by a temporary commission. Periodical appointments, however regulated, or by whomsoever made, would, in some way or other, be fatal to their necessary independence. If the power of making them was committed either to the Executive or legislature, there would be danger of an improper complaisance to the branch which possessed it; if to both, there would be an unwillingness to hazard the displeasure of either; if to the people, or to persons chosen by them for the special purpose, there would be too great a disposition to consult popularity, to justify a reliance that nothing would be consulted but the Constitution and the laws.

There is yet a further and a weightier reason for the permanency of the judicial offices, which is deducible from the nature of the qualifications they require. It has been frequently remarked, with great propriety, that a voluminous code of laws is one of the inconveniences necessarily connected with the advantages of a free government. To avoid an arbitrary discretion in the courts, it is indispensable that they should be bound down by strict rules and precedents, which serve to define and point out their duty in every particular case that comes before them; and it will readily be conceived from the variety of controversies which grow out of the folly and wickedness of mankind, that the records of those precedents must unavoidably swell to a very considerable bulk, and must demand long and laborious study to acquire a competent knowledge of them. Hence it is, that there can be but few men in the society who will have sufficient skill in the laws to qualify them for the stations of judges. And making the proper deductions for the ordinary depravity of human nature, the number must be still smaller of those who unite the requisite integrity with the requisite knowledge. These considerations apprise us, that the government can have no great option between fit character; and that a temporary duration in office, which would naturally discourage such characters from quitting a lucrative line of practice to accept a seat on the bench, would have a tendency to throw the administration of justice into hands less able, and less well qualified, to conduct it with utility and dignity. In the present circumstances of this country, and in those in which it is likely to be for a long time to come, the disadvantages on this score would be greater than they may at first sight appear; but it must be confessed, that they are far inferior to those which present themselves under the other aspects of the subject.

Upon the whole, there can be no room to doubt that the convention acted wisely in copying from the models of those constitutions which have established GOOD BEHAVIOR as the tenure of their judicial offices, in point of duration; and that so far from being blamable on this account, their plan would have been inexcusably defective, if it had wanted this important feature of good government. The experience of Great Britain affords an illustrious comment on the excellence of the institution.

PUBLIUS.

Outline of Federalist Paper No. 78

I. Introduction

A. Purpose of the paper

B. The importance of an independent judiciary

II. The Judiciary's Role and Independence

A. Judiciary as the weakest branch

B. The need for an independent judiciary to uphold the Constitution

C. Judiciary's role in checking the legislative and executive branches

III. Judicial Review

A. Judiciary's power of judicial review

B. The importance of interpreting and applying the Constitution

C. Judiciary's duty to strike down unconstitutional laws

IV. Tenure and Appointment of Judges

A. Life tenure for federal judges

B. Rationale behind life tenure to ensure judicial independence

C. The process of judicial appointments and confirmation

V. Judicial Restraint vs. Judicial Activism

A. The need for judges to exercise restraint and deference to the legislative branch

B. Balancing the interpretation of the law with safeguarding individual rights

VI. Protection Against Legislative Encroachments

A. Judiciary's role in preventing legislative encroachments on individual rights

B. The potential dangers of legislative power without proper checks

VII. Judicial Independence and Public Trust

A. The importance of public trust in the judiciary

B. Judiciary's role in maintaining the public's confidence in the government

VIII. Conclusion

A. Recap of the importance of an independent judiciary

B. Reiterating the need for a system of checks and balances

In Federalist Paper No. 78, Alexander Hamilton explains the judiciary's power of judicial review and its duty to interpret and apply the Constitution. Hamilton emphasizes the necessity of an independent judiciary to safeguard individual rights and check the potential abuses of the legislative and executive branches. He argues for the life tenure of federal judges to ensure their independence and addresses the balance between judicial restraint and activism. Hamilton also emphasizes the judiciary's role in protecting against legislative encroachments on individual rights and maintaining public trust in the government. Ultimately, he underscores the significance of a robust and independent judiciary within the system of checks and balances.

Brutus 1

To the Citizens of the State of New-York.

When the public is called to investigate and decide upon a question in which not only the present members of the community are deeply interested, but upon which the happiness and misery of generations yet unborn is in great measure suspended, the benevolent mind cannot help feeling itself peculiarly interested in the result.

In this situation, I trust the feeble efforts of an individual, to lead the minds of the people to a wise and prudent determination, cannot fail of being acceptable to the candid and dispassionate part of the community. Encouraged by this consideration, I have been induced to offer my thoughts upon the present important crisis of our public affairs.

Perhaps this country never saw so critical a period in their political concerns. We have felt the feebleness of the ties by which these United States are held together, and the want of sufficient energy in our present confederation, to manage, in some instances, our general concerns. Various expedients have been proposed to remedy these evils, but none have succeeded. At length a Convention of the states has been assembled, they have formed a constitution which will now, probably, be submitted to the people to ratify or reject, who are the fountain of all power, to whom alone it of right belongs to make or unmake constitutions, or forms of government, at their pleasure. The most important question that was ever proposed to your decision, or to the decision of any people under heaven, is before you, and you are to decide upon it by men of your own election, chosen specially for this purpose. If the constitution, offered to [your acceptance], be a wise one, calculated to preserve the invaluable blessings of liberty, to secure the inestimable rights of mankind, and promote human happiness, then, if you accept it, you will lay a lasting foundation of happiness for millions yet unborn; generations to come will rise up and call you blessed. You may rejoice in the prospects of this vast extended continent becoming filled with freemen, who will assert the dignity of human nature. You may solace yourselves with the idea, that society, in this favored land, will fast advance to the highest point of perfection; the human mind will expand in knowledge and virtue, and the golden age be, in some measure, realized. But if, on the other hand, this form of government contains principles that will lead to the subversion of liberty — if it tends to establish a despotism, or, what is worse, a tyrannic aristocracy; then, if you adopt it, this only remaining asylum for liberty will be [shut] up, and posterity will execrate your memory. . . .

With these few introductory remarks I shall proceed to a consideration of this constitution:

The first question that presents itself on the subject is, whether a confederated government be the best for the United States or not? Or in other words, whether the thirteen United States should be reduced to one great republic, governed by one legislature, and under the direction of one executive and judicial; or whether they should continue thirteen confederated republics, under the direction and control of a supreme federal head for certain defined national purposes only?

This inquiry is important, because, although the government reported by the convention does not go to a perfect and entire consolidation, yet it approaches so near to it, that it must, if executed, certainly and infallibly terminate in it.

This government is to possess absolute and uncontrollable power, legislative, executive and judicial, with respect to every object to which it extends, for by the last clause of section 8th, article 1st, it is declared "that the Congress shall have power to make all laws which shall be necessary and proper for carrying into execution the foregoing powers, and all other powers vested by this constitution, in the government of the United States; or in any department or office thereof." And by the 6th article, it is declared "that this constitution, and the laws of the United States, which shall be made in pursuance thereof, and the treaties made, or which shall be made, under the authority of the United States, shall be the supreme law of the land; and the judges in every state shall be bound thereby, any thing in the constitution, or law of any state to the contrary notwithstanding." It appears from these articles that there is no need of any intervention of the state governments, between the Congress and the people, to execute any one power vested in the general government, and that the constitution and laws of every state are nullified and declared void, so far as they are or shall be inconsistent with this constitution, or the laws made in pursuance of it, or with treaties made under the authority of the United States. — The government then, so far as it extends, is a complete one, and not a confederation. It is as much one complete government as that of New-York or Massachusetts, has as absolute and perfect powers to make and execute all laws, to appoint officers, institute courts, declare offences, and annex penalties, with respect to every object to which it extends, as any other in the world. So far therefore as its powers reach, all ideas of confederation are given up and lost. It is true this government is limited to certain objects, or to speak more properly, some small degree of power is still left to the states, but a little attention to the powers vested in the general government, will convince every candid man, that if it is capable of being executed, all that is reserved for the individual states must very soon be annihilated, except so far as they are barely necessary to the organization of the general government. The powers of the general legislature extend to every case that is of the least importance — there is nothing valuable to human nature, nothing dear to freemen, but what is within its power. It has authority to make laws which will affect the lives, the liberty, and property of every man in the United States; nor can the constitution or laws of any state, in any way prevent or impede the full and complete execution of every power given. The legislative power is competent to lay taxes, duties, imposts, and excises; — there is no limitation to this power, unless it be said that the clause which directs the use to which those taxes, and duties shall be applied, may be said to be a limitation; but this is no restriction of the power at all, for by this clause they are to be applied to pay the debts and provide for the common defense and general welfare of the United States; but the legislature have authority to contract debts at their discretion; they are the sole judges of what is necessary to provide for the common defense, and they only are to determine what is for the general welfare: this power therefore is neither more nor less, than a power to lay and collect taxes, imposts, and excises, at their pleasure; not only the power to lay taxes unlimited, as to the amount they may require, but it is perfect and absolute to raise them in any mode they please. No state legislature, or any power in the state governments, have any more to do in carrying this into effect, than the authority of one state has to do with that of another. In the business therefore of laying and collecting taxes, the idea of confederation is totally lost, and that of one entire republic is embraced. It is proper here to remark, that the authority to lay and collect taxes is the most important of any power that can be granted; it connects with it almost all other powers, or at least will in process of time draw all other after it; it is the great mean of protection, security, and defense, in a good government, and the great engine of oppression and tyranny in a bad one. This cannot fail of being the case, if we consider the contracted limits which are set by this constitution, to the late governments, on this article of raising money. No state can emit paper money — lay any duties, or imposts, on imports, or exports, but by consent of the Congress; and then the net produce shall be for the benefit of the United States. The only mean therefore left, for any state to support its government and discharge its debts, is by direct taxation; and the United States have also power to lay and collect taxes, in any way they please. Every one who has thought on the subject, must be convinced that but small sums of money can be collected in any country, by direct taxes[; hence,] when the federal government begins to exercise the right of taxation in all its parts, the legislatures of the several states will find it impossible to raise monies to support their governments. Without money they cannot be supported, and they must dwindle away, and, as before observed, their powers [will be] absorbed in that of the general government.

It might be here shown, that the power in the federal legislative, to raise and support armies at pleasure, as well in peace as in war, and their control over the militia, tend, not only to a consolidation of the government, but the destruction of liberty. — I shall not, however, dwell upon these, as a few observations upon the judicial power of this government, in addition to the preceding, will fully evince the truth of the position.

The judicial power of the United States is to be vested in a supreme court, and in such inferior courts as Congress may from time to time ordain and establish. The powers of these courts are very extensive; their jurisdiction comprehends all civil causes, except such as arise between citizens of the same state; and it extends to all cases in law and equity arising under the constitution. One inferior court must be established, I presume, in each state at least, with the necessary executive officers appendant thereto. It is easy to see, that in the common course of things, these courts will eclipse the dignity, and take away from the respectability, of the state courts. These courts will be, in themselves, totally independent of the states, deriving their authority from the United States, and receiving from them fixed salaries; and in the course of human events it is to be expected, that they will swallow up all the powers of the courts in the respective states.

How far the clause in the 8th section of the 1st article may operate to do away all idea of confederated states, and to effect an entire consolidation of the whole into one general government, it is impossible to say. The powers given by this article are very general and comprehensive, and it may receive a construction to justify the passing almost any law. A power to make all laws, which shall be necessary and proper, for carrying into execution, all powers vested by the constitution in the government of the United States, or any department or officer thereof, is a power very comprehensive and definite, and may, for ought I know, be exercised in a such manner as entirely to abolish the state legislatures. Suppose the legislature of a state should pass a law to raise money to support their government and pay the state debt, may the Congress repeal this law, because it may prevent the collection of a tax which they may think proper and necessary to lay, to provide for the general welfare of the United States? For all laws made, in pursuance of this constitution, are the supreme law of the land, and the judges in every state shall be bound thereby, any thing in the constitution or laws of the different states to the contrary notwithstanding. — By such a law, the government of a particular state might be overturned at one stroke, and thereby be deprived of every means of its support.

It is not meant, by stating this case, to insinuate that the constitution would warrant a law of this kind; or unnecessarily to alarm the fears of the people, by suggesting, that the federal legislature would be more likely to pass the limits assigned them by the constitution, than that of an individual state, further than they are less responsible to the people. But what is meant is, that the legislature of the United States are vested with the great and uncontrollable powers, of laying and collecting taxes, duties, imposts, and excises; of regulating trade, raising and supporting armies, organizing, arming, and disciplining the militia, instituting courts, and other general powers. And are by this clause invested with the power of making all laws, proper and necessary, for carrying all these into execution; and they may so exercise this power as entirely to annihilate all the state governments, and reduce this country to one single government. And if they may do it, it is pretty certain they will; for it will be found that the power retained by individual states, small as it is, will be a clog upon the wheels of the government of the United States; the latter therefore will be naturally inclined to remove it out of the way. Besides, it is a truth confirmed by the unerring experience of ages, that every man, and every body of men, invested with power, are ever disposed to increase it, and to acquire a superiority over every thing that stands in their way. This disposition, which is implanted in human nature, will operate in the federal legislature to lessen and ultimately to subvert the state authority, and having such advantages, will most certainly succeed, if the federal government succeeds at all. It must be very evident then, that what this constitution wants of being a complete consolidation of the several parts of the union into one complete government, possessed of perfect legislative, judicial, and executive powers, to all intents and purposes, it will necessarily acquire in its exercise and operation.

Let us now proceed to inquire, as I at first proposed, whether it be best the thirteen United States should be reduced to one great republic, or not? It is here taken for granted, that all agree in this, that whatever government we adopt, it ought to be a free one; that it should be so framed as to secure the liberty of the citizens of America, and such an one as to admit of a full, fair, and equal representation of the people. The question then will be, whether a government thus constituted, and founded on such principles, is practicable, and can be exercised over the whole United States, reduced into one state?

If respect is to be paid to the opinion of the greatest and wisest men who have ever thought or wrote on the science of government, we shall be constrained to conclude, that a free republic cannot succeed over a country of such immense extent, containing such a number of inhabitants, and these increasing in such rapid progression as that of the whole United States. Among the many illustrious authorities which might be produced to this point, I shall content myself with quoting only two.

The one is the Baron de Montesquieu, Spirit of the Laws,[1] Chap. xvi. Vol. I [Book VIII]. "It is natural to a republic to have only a small territory, otherwise it cannot long subsist. In a large republic there are men of large fortunes, and consequently of less moderation; there are trusts too great to be placed in any single subject; he has interest of his own; he soon begins to think that he may be happy, great and glorious, by oppressing his fellow citizens; and that he may raise himself to grandeur on the ruins of his country. In a large republic, the public good is sacrificed to a thousand views; it is subordinate to exceptions, and depends on accidents. In a small one, the interest of the public is easier perceived, better understood, and more within the reach of every citizen; abuses are of less extent, and of course are less protected." Of the same opinion is the Marquis Beccarari.[2]

History furnishes no example of a free republic, anything like the extent of the United States. The Grecian republics were of small extent; so also was that of the Romans. Both of these, it is true, in process of time, extended their conquests over large territories of country; and the consequence was, that their governments were changed from that of free governments to those of the most tyrannical that ever existed in the world.

Not only the opinion of the greatest men, and the experience of mankind, are against the idea of an extensive republic, but a variety of reasons may be drawn from the reason and nature of things, against it. In every government, the will of the sovereign is the law. In despotic governments, the supreme authority being lodged in one, his will is law, and can be as easily expressed to a large extensive territory as to a small one. In a pure democracy the people are the sovereign, and their will is declared by themselves; for this purpose they must all come together to deliberate, and decide.

This kind of government cannot be exercised, therefore, over a country of any considerable extent; it must be confined to a single city, or at least limited to such bounds as that the people can conveniently assemble, be able to debate, understand the subject submitted to them, and declare their opinion concerning it.

In a free republic, although all laws are derived from the consent of the people, yet the people do not declare their consent by themselves in person, but by representatives, chosen by them, who are supposed to know the minds of their constituents, and to be possessed of integrity to declare this mind.

In every free government, the people must give their assent to the laws by which they are governed. This is the true criterion between a free government and an arbitrary one. The former are ruled by the will of the whole, expressed in any manner they may agree upon; the latter by the will of one, or a few. If the people are to give their assent to the laws, by persons chosen and appointed by them, the manner of the choice and the number chosen, must be such, as to possess, be disposed, and consequently qualified to declare the sentiments of the people; for if they do not know, or are not disposed to speak the sentiments of the people, the people do not govern, but the sovereignty is in a few. Now, in a large extended country, it is impossible to have a representation, possessing the sentiments, and of integrity, to declare the minds of the people, without having it so numerous and unwieldy, as to be subject in great measure to the inconveniency of a democratic government.

The territory of the United States is of vast extent; it now contains near three millions of souls, and is capable of containing much more than ten times that number. Is it practicable for a country, so large and so numerous as they will soon become, to elect a representation, that will speak their sentiments, without their becoming so numerous as to be incapable of transacting public business? It certainly is not.

In a republic, the manners, sentiments, and interests of the people should be similar. If this be not the case, there will be a constant clashing of opinions; and the representatives of one part will be continually striving against those of the other. This will retard the operations of government, and prevent such conclusions as will promote the public good. If we apply this remark to the condition of the United States, we shall be convinced that it forbids that we should be one government. The United States includes a variety of climates. The productions of the different parts of the union are very variant, and their interests, of consequence, diverse. Their manners and habits differ as much as their climates and productions; and their sentiments are by no means coincident. The laws and customs of the several states are, in many respects, very diverse, and in some opposite; each would be in favor of its own interests and customs, and, of consequence, a legislature, formed of representatives from the respective parts, would not only be too numerous to act with any care or decision, but would be composed of such heterogeneous and discordant principles, as would constantly be contending with each other.

The laws cannot be executed in a republic, of an extent equal to that of the United States, with promptitude.

The magistrates in every government must be supported in the execution of the laws, either by an armed force, maintained at the public expense for that purpose; or by the people turning out to aid the magistrate upon his command, in case of resistance.

In despotic governments, as well as in all the monarchies of Europe, standing armies are kept up to execute the commands of the prince or the magistrate, and are employed for this purpose when occasion requires: But they have always proved the destruction of liberty, and [are] abhorrent to the spirit of a free republic. In England, where they depend upon the parliament for their annual support, they have always been complained of as oppressive and unconstitutional, and are seldom employed in executing of the laws; never except on extraordinary occasions, and then under the direction of a civil magistrate.

A free republic will never keep a standing army to execute its laws. It must depend upon the support of its citizens. But when a government is to receive its support from the aid of the citizens, it must be so constructed as to have the confidence, respect, and affection of the people. Men who, upon the call of the magistrate, offer themselves to execute the laws, are influenced to do it either by affection to the government, or from fear; where a standing army is at hand to punish offenders, every man is actuated by the latter principle, and therefore, when the magistrate calls, will obey: but, where this is not the case, the government must rest for its support upon the confidence and respect which the people have for their government and laws. The body of the people being attached, the government will always be sufficient to support and execute its laws, and to operate upon the fears of any faction which may be opposed to it, not only to prevent an opposition to the execution of the laws themselves, but also to compel the most of them to aid the magistrate; but the people will not be likely to have such confidence in their rulers, in a republic so extensive as the United States, as necessary for these purposes. The confidence which the people have in their rulers, in a free republic, arises from their knowing them, from their being responsible to them for their conduct, and from the power they have of displacing them when they misbehave: but in a republic of the extent of this continent, the people in general would be acquainted with very few of their rulers: the people at large would know little of their proceedings, and it would be extremely difficult to change them. The people in Georgia and New-Hampshire would not know one another's mind, and therefore could not act in concert to enable them to effect a general change of representatives. The different parts of so extensive a country could not possibly be made acquainted with the conduct of their representatives, nor be informed of the reasons upon which measures were founded. The consequence will be, they will have no confidence in their legislature, suspect them of ambitious views, be jealous of every measure they adopt, and will not support the laws they pass. Hence the government will be nerveless and inefficient, and no way will be left to render it otherwise, but by establishing an armed force to execute the laws at the point of the bayonet — a government of all others the most to be dreaded.

In a republic of such vast extent as the United-States, the legislature cannot attend to the various concerns and wants of its different parts. It cannot be sufficiently numerous to be acquainted with the local condition and wants of the different districts, and if it could, it is impossible it should have sufficient time to attend to and provide for all the variety of cases of this nature, that would be continually arising.

In so extensive a republic, the great officers of government would soon become above the control of the people, and abuse their power to the purpose of aggrandizing themselves, and oppressing them. The trust committed to the executive offices, in a country of the extent of the United-States, must be various and of magnitude. The command of all the troops and navy of the republic, the appointment of officers, the power of pardoning offences, the collecting of all the public revenues, and the power of expending them, with a number of other powers, must be lodged and exercised in every state, in the hands of a few. When these are attended with great honor and emolument, as they always will be in large states, so as greatly to interest men to pursue them, and to be proper objects for ambitious and designing men, such men will be ever restless in their pursuit after them. They will use the power, when they have acquired it, to the purposes of gratifying their own interest and ambition, and it is scarcely possible, in a very large republic, to call them to account for their misconduct, or to prevent their abuse of power.

These are some of the reasons by which it appears, that a free republic cannot long subsist over a country of the great extent of these states. If then this new constitution is calculated to consolidate the thirteen states into one, as it evidently is, it ought not to be adopted.

Though I am of opinion, that it is a sufficient objection to this government, to reject it, that it creates the whole union into one government, under the form of a republic, yet if this objection was obviated, there are exceptions to it, which are so material and fundamental, that they ought to determine every man, who is a friend to the liberty and happiness of mankind, not to adopt it. I beg the candid and dispassionate attention of my countrymen while I state these objections — they are such as have obtruded themselves upon my mind upon a careful attention to the matter, and such as I sincerely believe are well founded. There are many objections, of small moment, of which I shall take no notice — perfection is not to be expected in any thing that is the production of man — and if I did not in my conscience believe that this scheme was defective in the fundamental principles — in the foundation upon which a free and equal government must rest — I would hold my peace.

Brutus.

Outline of Brutus 1

I. Introduction

   A. Opening statement: The essay aims to provide a critical analysis of the proposed Constitution.

   B. Author's identification as Brutus, borrowing from the Roman senator who opposed the rise of Julius Caesar.

II. Concerns about Consolidation of Power

   A. Fear of centralization: Expresses concerns that the Constitution grants too much power to the federal government, leading to the consolidation of power and potential tyranny.

   B. Comparison to the British system: Highlights the dangers of centralized power and how it can subvert individual liberties.

III. State Sovereignty

   A. Importance of state governments: Argues that the Constitution diminishes the sovereignty of individual states and undermines their ability to protect their citizens' rights and interests.

   B. Fears of federal encroachment: Suggests that a powerful federal government could infringe upon state authority, leading to an imbalance of power and reduced representation.

IV. Size and Scope of the Republic

   A. The dangers of a large republic: Asserts that a republic as extensive as the United States would be difficult to govern effectively, rendering the representation of citizens insufficient and distant from their concerns.

   B. Advocacy for a smaller republic: Supports the idea of smaller, more localized governments that are closer to the people and better able to protect individual liberties.

V. The Necessary and Proper Clause and the Supremacy Clause

   A. Concerns over expansive interpretation: Criticizes the broad language of the Necessary and Proper Clause, which could potentially lead to the expansion of federal power beyond its intended scope.

   B. Critique of the Supremacy Clause: Raises concerns about the Supremacy Clause's potential to undermine state sovereignty and subject state laws to federal authority.

VI. Fear of a Standing Army

   A. Potential for military tyranny: Expresses apprehension about the presence of a standing army, which could be used by the federal government to suppress the liberties of the people and potentially lead to military despotism.

   B. Historical examples: Draws upon historical instances where standing armies were used to undermine individual freedoms and oppress citizens.

VII. Lack of a Bill of Rights

   A. Absence of explicit guarantees: Expresses unease about the absence of a Bill of Rights within the Constitution, arguing that individual liberties must be explicitly protected from potential government encroachment.

   B. Potential for government abuse: Believes that without a Bill of Rights, the federal government could infringe upon citizens' rights, including freedom of speech, religion, and due process.

VIII. Conclusion

   A. Restatement of concerns: Reiterates the dangers of a powerful federal government and the need for strong protections of individual liberties.

   B. Call to action: Urges citizens to reject the Constitution in its current form and instead advocate for amendments that better safeguard individual rights, limit federal power, and address concerns regarding a standing army.

Letter from Birmingham Jail

Dr. Martin Luther King, Jr.

April 16, 1963

My Dear Fellow Clergymen,
While confined here in the Birmingham City Jail, I came across your recent statement calling our present activities "unwise and untimely." Seldom, if ever, do I pause to answer criticism of my work and ideas … But since I feel that you are men of genuine good will and your criticisms are sincerely set forth, I would like to answer your statement in what I hope will be patient and reasonable terms.

I think I should give the reason for my being in Birmingham, since you have been influenced by the argument of "outsiders coming in." I have the honor of serving as president of the Southern Christian Leadership Conference, an organization operating in every Southern state with headquarters in Atlanta, Georgia. We have some 85 affiliate organizations all across the South … Several months ago our local affiliate here in Birmingham invited us to be on call to engage in a nonviolent direct action program if such were deemed necessary. We readily consented.

In any nonviolent campaign there are four basic steps: 1) collection of the facts to determine whether injustices are alive; 2) negotiation; 3) self-purification; and 4) direct action. We have gone through all of these steps in Birmingham … Birmingham is probably the most thoroughly segregated city in the United States. Its ugly record of police brutality is known in every section of the country. Its unjust treatment of Negroes in the courts is a notorious reality. There have been more unsolved bombings of Negro homes and churches in Birmingham than in any city in this nation. These are the hard, brutal, and unbelievable facts. On the basis of these conditions Negro leaders sought to negotiate with the city fathers. But the political leaders consistently refused to engage in good faith negotiation.

Then came the opportunity last September to talk with some of the leaders of the economic community. In these negotiating sessions certain promises were made by the merchants—such as the promise to remove the humiliating racial signs from the stores. On the basis of these promises Reverend Shuttlesworth and the leaders of the Alabama Christian Movement for Human Rights agreed to call a moratorium on any type of demonstrations. As the weeks and months unfolded we realized that we were the victims of a broken promise. The signs remained. As in so many experiences in the past, we were confronted with blasted hopes, and the dark shadow of a deep disappointment settled upon us. So we had no alternative except that of preparing for direct action, whereby we would present our very bodies as a means of laying our case before the conscience of the local and national community. We were not unmindful of the difficulties involved. So we decided to go through the process of self-purification. We started having workshops on nonviolence and repeatedly asked ourselves the questions, "are you able to accept the blows without retaliating?" "Are you able to endure the ordeals of jail?"

You may well ask, "Why direct action? Why sit-ins, marches, etc.? Isn't negotiation a better path?" You are exactly right in your call for negotiation. Indeed, this is the purpose of direct action. Nonviolent direct action seeks to create such a crisis and establish such creative tension that a community that has constantly refused to negotiate is forced to confront the issue.

My friends, I must say to you that we have not made a single gain in civil rights without legal and nonviolent pressure. History is the long and tragic story of the fact that privileged groups seldom give up their privileges voluntarily. Individuals may see the moral light and give up their unjust posture; but as Reinhold Niebuhr has reminded us, groups are more immoral than individuals.

We know through painful experience that freedom is never voluntarily given by the oppressor; it must be demanded by the oppressed. Frankly I have never yet engaged in a direct action movement that was "well timed," according to the timetable of those who have not suffered unduly from the disease of segregation. For years now I have heard the word "Wait!" It rings in the ear of every Negro with a piercing familiarity. This "wait" has almost always meant "never." It has been a tranquilizing Thalidomide, relieving the emotional stress for a moment, only to give birth to an ill-formed infant of frustration. We must come to see with the distinguished jurist of yesterday that "justice too long delayed is justice denied." We have waited for more than 340 years for our constitutional and God-given rights. The nations of Asia and Africa are moving with jetlike speed toward the goal of political independence, and we still creep at horse and buggy pace toward the gaining of a cup of coffee at a lunch counter.

I guess it is easy for those who have never felt the stinging darts of segregation to say wait. But when you have seen vicious mobs lynch your mothers and fathers at will and drown your sisters and brothers at whim; when you have seen hate-filled policemen curse, kick, brutalize, and even kill your black brothers and sisters with impunity; when you see the vast majority of your 20 million Negro brothers smothering in an airtight cage of poverty in the midst of an affluent society; when you suddenly find your tongue twisted and your speech stammering as you seek to explain to your six-year-old daughter why she can't go to the public amusement park that has just been advertised on television, and see the tears welling up in her little eyes when she is told that Funtown is closed to colored children, and see the depressing clouds of inferiority begin to form in her little mental sky, and see her begin to distort her little personality by unconsciously developing a bitterness toward white people; when you have to concoct an answer for a five-year-old son who is asking in agonizing pathos: "Daddy, why do white people treat colored people so mean?" when you take a cross country drive and find it necessary to sleep night after night in the uncomfortable corners of your automobile because no motel will accept you; when you are humiliated day in and day out by nagging signs reading "white" men and "colored" when your first name becomes "nigger" and your middle name becomes "boy" (however old you are) and your last name becomes "John," and when your wife and mother are never given the respected title of "Mrs." when you are harried by day and haunted by night by the fact that you are a Negro, living constantly at tip-toe stance, never quite knowing what to expect next, and plagued with inner fears and outer resentments; when you are forever fighting a degenerating sense of "nobodiness"—then you will understand why we find it difficult to wait. There comes a time when the cup of endurance runs over, and men are no longer willing to be plunged into an abyss of injustice where they experience the bleakness of corroding despair. I hope, sirs, you can understand our legitimate and unavoidable impatience.

I must make two honest confessions to you, my Christian and Jewish brothers. First, I must confess that over the last few years I have been gravely disappointed with the white moderate. I have almost reached the regrettable conclusion that the Negro's great stumbling block in the stride toward freedom is not the White citizens' "Councilor" or the Ku Klux Klanner, but the white moderate who is more devoted to "order" than to justice; who prefers a negative peace which is the absence of tension to a positive peace which is the presence of justice; who constantly says "I agree with you in the goal you seek, but I can't agree with your methods of direst action" who paternistically feels that he can set the timetable for another man's freedom; who lives by the myth of time and who constantly advises the Negro to wait until a "more convenient season." Shallow understanding from people of good will is more frustrating than absolute misunderstanding from people of ill will. Lukewarm acceptance is much more bewildering than outright rejection.

You spoke of our activity in Birmingham as extreme. At first I was rather disappointed that fellow clergymen would see my nonviolent efforts as those of an extremist. I started thinking about the fact that I stand in the middle of two opposing forces in the Negro community. One is a force of complacency made up of Negroes who, as a result of long years of oppression, have been so completely drained of self-respect and a sense of "somebodiness" that they have adjusted to segregation, and a few Negroes in the middle class who, because of a degree of academic and economic security, and at points they profit from segregation, have unconsciously become insensitive to the problems of the masses. The other force is one of bitterness and hatred and comes perilously close to advocating violence. It is expressed in the various black nationalist groups that are springing up over the nation, the largest and best known being Elijah Muhammad's Muslim movement. This movement is nourished by the contemporary frustration over the continued existence of racial discrimination. It is made up of people who have lost faith in America, who have absolutely repudiated Christianity, and who have concluded that the white man in an incurable "devil."

The Negro has many pent-up resentments and latent frustrations. He has to get them out. So let him march sometime; let him have his prayer pilgrimages to the city hall; understand why he must have sit-ins and freedom rides. If his repressed emotions do not come out in these nonviolent ways, they will come out in ominous expressions of violence. This is not a threat; it is a fact of history. So I have not said to my people, "Get rid of your discontent." But I have tried to say that this normal and healthy discontent can be channeled through the creative outlet of nonviolent direct action.

In spite of my shattered dreams of the past, I came to Birmingham with the hope that the white religious leadership in the community would see the justice of our cause and, with deep moral concern, serve as the channel through which our just grievances could get to the power structure. I had hoped that each of you would understand. But again I have been disappointed. I have heard numerous religious leaders of the South call upon their worshippers to comply with a desegregation decision because it is the law, but I have longed to hear white ministers say follow this decree because integration is morally right and the Negro is your brother. In the midst of blatant injustices inflicted upon the Negro, I have watched white churches stand on the sideline and merely mouth pious irrelevancies and sanctimonious trivialities. In the midst of a mighty struggle to rid our nation of racial and economic injustice, I have heard so many ministers say, "Those are social issues with which the Gospel has no real concern," and I have watched so many churches commit themselves to a completely other-worldly religion which made a strange distinction between body and soul, the sacred and the secular.

I hope this letter finds you strong in the faith. I also hope that circumstances will soon make it possible for me to meet each of you, not as an integrationist or a civil rights leader, but as a fellow clergyman and a Christian brother. Let us all hope that the dark clouds of racial prejudice will soon pass away and the deep fog of misunderstanding will be lifted from our fear-drenched communities and in some not too distant tomorrow the radiant stars of love and brotherhood will shine over our great nation with all of their scintillating beauty.

Yours for the cause of Peace and Brotherhood,

M. L. King, Jr.

Outline of Martin Luther King Jr.'s "Letter from Birmingham Jail":

I. Introduction
   A. Background and context: King's letter written in response to a published statement by eight Alabama clergymen criticizing the civil rights protests in Birmingham.

   B. Purpose and audience: King's letter addresses the clergymen's concerns while explaining the motivations and justifications for the civil rights movement.

II. Exposition of Nonviolent Direct Action
   A. Definition and principles of nonviolent direct action: King explains the philosophy and methodology behind nonviolent protest as a means to bring attention to racial injustice.

   B. Justification for direct action: King argues that nonviolent direct action is necessary when negotiations and legal channels have failed to address systemic racism.

III. Critique of Injustice and Segregation
   A. Moral obligation to fight injustice: King discusses the moral imperative to combat racial inequality and segregation, emphasizing the importance of challenging unjust laws.

   B. Effects of segregation on African Americans: King describes the profound impact of segregation on African American communities and individuals, highlighting its dehumanizing and oppressive nature.

IV. Response to Critics and Moderates
   A. Addressing the criticism of timing: King defends the timing of the civil rights protests and explains the urgency for immediate action against racial injustice.

   B. Critique of white moderates: King responds to the clergymen's call for patience, highlighting the detrimental role of white moderates who prefer order over justice.

V. The Interconnectedness of Justice
   A. Interrelatedness of communities: King emphasizes the interconnectedness of all communities, stating that injustice anywhere is a threat to justice everywhere.

B. Call for unity: King encourages individuals from all racial and religious backgrounds to unite in the fight against discrimination and inequality.

VI. The Power of Nonviolent Resistance

A. Historical examples of successful nonviolent movements: King cites examples of successful nonviolent resistance, such as the Montgomery Bus Boycott, to demonstrate the effectiveness of peaceful protest.

B. The redemptive power of love: King highlights the transformative and redemptive nature of nonviolence, appealing to the conscience of oppressors and promoting reconciliation.

VII. Conclusion

A. Hope for the future: King expresses optimism that the civil rights movement will ultimately triumph over racial injustice.

B. Call to action: King urges readers to join the struggle for freedom, equality, and justice, emphasizing the importance of nonviolent resistance in achieving these goals.

Note: This outline provides a general structure for "Letter from Birmingham Jail." The actual letter contains a rich and nuanced exploration of these themes and may include additional arguments, examples, and rhetorical devices.

Comparison and connection between the Declaration of Independence and Martin Luther King Jr.'s "Letter from Birmingham Jail"

Declaration of Independence:
"We hold these truths to be self-evident, that all men are created equal, that they are endowed by their Creator with certain unalienable Rights, that among these are Life, Liberty and the pursuit of Happiness." (Declaration of Independence)

"Letter from Birmingham Jail":
"Injustice anywhere is a threat to justice everywhere." (Martin Luther King Jr., "Letter from Birmingham Jail")

Connection: Both the Declaration of Independence and King's letter emphasize the fundamental belief in the inherent equality and rights of all individuals. The Declaration proclaims that all people are created equal and have the unalienable rights of life, liberty, and the pursuit of happiness. Similarly, King's letter echoes this sentiment, emphasizing the interconnectedness of justice and highlighting that injustice anywhere is a threat to justice everywhere. Both documents stress the importance of recognizing and protecting the rights and dignity of every individual, irrespective of race or social status.

Declaration of Independence:
"That whenever any Form of Government becomes destructive of these ends, it is the Right of the People to alter or to abolish it, and to institute new Government." (Declaration of Independence)

"Letter from Birmingham Jail":
"One has not only a legal, but a moral responsibility to obey just laws. Conversely, one has a moral responsibility to disobey unjust laws." (Martin Luther King Jr., "Letter from Birmingham Jail")

Both the Declaration and King's letter emphasize the importance of challenging and confronting unjust systems of governance. The Declaration asserts the right of the people to alter or abolish a government that becomes destructive of their rights and freedoms. Similarly, King argues that individuals have a moral obligation to disobey unjust laws and fight against systems that perpetuate injustice. Both documents advocate for active engagement in the pursuit of justice and the willingness to challenge and change oppressive structures.

CASE BRIEF FORMS (15)

Marbury v. Madison (1803)

Legal Issue(s):

Facts of the Case:

Procedural History:

Majority Opinion:

Concurring Opinion(s):

Dissenting Opinion(s):

Legal Reasoning:

Impact/Significance of the Case:

McCulloch v. Maryland (1819)

Legal Issue(s):

Facts of the Case:

Procedural History:

Majority Opinion:

Concurring Opinion(s):

Dissenting Opinion(s):

Legal Reasoning:

Impact/Significance of the Case:

Schenck v. the United States (1919)

Legal Issue(s):

Facts of the Case:

Procedural History:

Majority Opinion:

Concurring Opinion(s):

Dissenting Opinion(s):

Legal Reasoning:

Impact/Significance of the Case:

Brown v. Board of Education (1954)

Legal Issue(s):

Facts of the Case:

Procedural History:

Majority Opinion:

Concurring Opinion(s):

Dissenting Opinion(s):

Legal Reasoning:

Impact/Significance of the Case:

Engel v. Vitale (1962)

Legal Issue(s):

Facts of the Case:

Procedural History:

Majority Opinion:

Concurring Opinion(s):

Dissenting Opinion(s):

Legal Reasoning:

Impact/Significance of the Case:

Baker v. Carr (1962)

Legal Issue(s):

Facts of the Case:

Procedural History:

Majority Opinion:

Concurring Opinion(s):

Dissenting Opinion(s):

Legal Reasoning:

Impact/Significance of the Case:

Gideon v. Wainwright (1963)

Legal Issue(s):

Facts of the Case:

Procedural History:

Majority Opinion:

Concurring Opinion(s):

Dissenting Opinion(s):

Legal Reasoning:

Impact/Significance of the Case:

Tinker v. Des Moines Independent Community School District
(1969)

Legal Issue(s):

Facts of the Case:

Procedural History:

Majority Opinion:

Concurring Opinion(s):

Dissenting Opinion(s):

Legal Reasoning:

Impact/Significance of the Case:

New York Times Co. v. United States (1971)

Legal Issue(s):

Facts of the Case:

Procedural History:

Majority Opinion:

Concurring Opinion(s):

Dissenting Opinion(s):

Legal Reasoning:

Impact/Significance of the Case:

Wisconsin v. Yoder (1972)

Legal Issue(s):

Facts of the Case:

Procedural History:

Majority Opinion:

Concurring Opinion(s):

Dissenting Opinion(s):

Legal Reasoning:

Impact/Significance of the Case:

Shaw v. Reno (1993)

Legal Issue(s):

Facts of the Case:

Procedural History:

Majority Opinion:

Concurring Opinion(s):

Dissenting Opinion(s):

Legal Reasoning:

Impact/Significance of the Case:

United States v. Lopez (1995)

Legal Issue(s):

Facts of the Case:

Procedural History:

Majority Opinion:

Concurring Opinion(s):

Dissenting Opinion(s):

Legal Reasoning:

Impact/Significance of the Case:

McDonald v. Chicago (2010)

Legal Issue(s):

Facts of the Case:

Procedural History:

Majority Opinion:

Concurring Opinion(s):

Dissenting Opinion(s):

Legal Reasoning:

Impact/Significance of the Case:

Citizens United v. Federal Election Commission (2010)

Legal Issue(s):

Facts of the Case:

Procedural History:

Majority Opinion:

Concurring Opinion(s):

Dissenting Opinion(s):

Legal Reasoning:

Impact/Significance of the Case:

Roe v. Wade (1973)

Legal Issue(s):

Facts of the Case:

Procedural History:

Majority Opinion:

Concurring Opinion(s):

Dissenting Opinion(s):

Legal Reasoning:

NOTES